Student Notebook – Fourth Grade

ISBN: 978-1-63037-597-3

Published by Accelerate Learning Inc., 5177 Richmond Ave, Suite 1025, Houston, TX 77056.

To learn more, visit us at www.stemscopes.com.

10 9 8 7 6 5 4 3 2

This Student Notebook is designed to be used as a companion piece to our online curriculum.

The pages of this book are organized and follow the 5E model.

ENGAGE

Student Handout

A short activity to grab students' interest

EXPLORE

Student Journal

Hands-on tasks, including scientific investigations, engineering solutions, and problem-based learning (PBL)

Claim-Evidence-Reasoning (CER)

A formative assessment in which students write a scientific explanation to show their understanding

EXPLAIN

Linking Literacy

Strategies to help students comprehend difficult informational text

ELABORATE

Reading Science

A reading passage about the concept that includes comprehension questions

EVALUATE

Claim-Evidence-Reasoning (CER)

A summative assessment in which students write a scientific explanation to show their understanding

Open-Ended Response (OER)

A short answer and essay assessment to evaluate mastery of the concept

Only student pages are included in this book, and directions on how to use these pages are found in our online curriculum. Use the URL address and password provided to you by your district to access our full curriculum.

Student Notebook - Fourth Grade
Table of Contents

Lesson | Page

Name: _____

Date: _____

California Instructional Segment

Mission Log

Mission Log

Anchoring Phenomena

What happens to energy during a car crash?

Mission Briefing

You have gotten a job at the ALI Car Company in its race car division. You will consider current safety features and then design a new feature to lessen the impact of energy transferred during a crash, which will increase the chance of survival for the driver.

- Why do car crashes cause so much damage?

- Why is the driver affected by a crash if the collision happens to the car?

California Instructional Segment

Mission Log

Class Mission Log

Information Gained

Energy and Speed

What happens to an object if more force is applied?

_____

Will all objects move when a force is applied? Why or why not?

_____

_____

Transfer of Energy in Collision

Do objects need to touch in order to have a collision?

_____

_____

What happens to energy when objects collide?

_____

_____

Connection to Mission

Energy and Speed

List some safety features that protect the driver in a low-impact collision.

_____

Why are more features needed for higher-impact crashes?

_____

_____

Transfer of Energy in Collision

How is the energy of a crash transferred to the driver?

_____

_____

Why are airbags used to protect the driver during a collision? Can you think of anything else that could be used in the same way?

_____

_____

California Instructional Segment

Action Plan

Action Plan

Create a new safety feature to keep a race car driver safe during a collision. It can be inside or outside the car.

Here's what we know:

- The greater the force that is applied, the greater the reaction is.

- Energy is transferred during a collision.

- Energy can travel through objects and cause change, even without direct contact.

- When there is no change in the motion, the forces are balanced; unbalanced forces mean a change in motion will happen.

- The race car already has a seat belt and airbags to protect the driver.

![California logo]

California Instructional Segment
Action Plan

Take Action

Design a new safety feature to protect your race car driver. It should be light enough that it does not slow down the car but is still effective. Draw your car below with the new safety feature. Describe how this feature will help keep the driver safe.

Energy and Speed

Graphic Organizer

How Speed Affects Energy

Directions

Write an example of a moving object in the box (e.g., dogs running, cars colliding, etc.). If the object's speed increases or decreases, write whether the object will possess more energy or less energy.

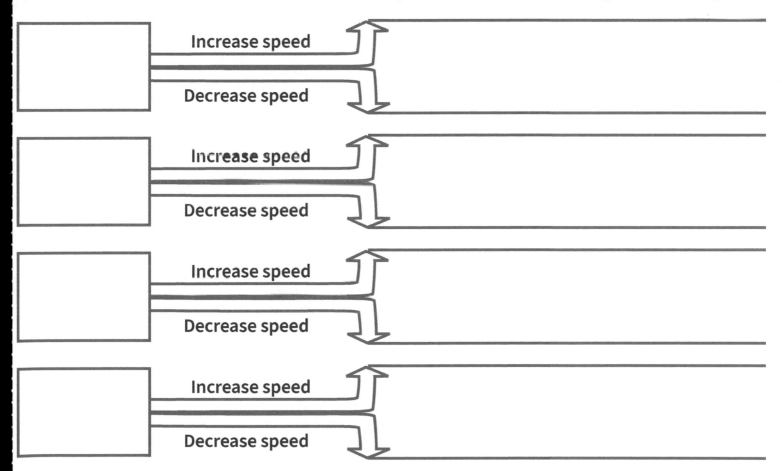

What pattern do you notice with speed and energy of objects?

_____

_____

_____

🔍 Explore 1

Racing for Distance

Our Driving Question

How does the height of a ramp affect the collision of objects?

What We Need

1 Golf ball	1 Large jingle bell
1 Board (small, dry erase)	1 Dry-erase marker
1 Meterstick	1 Masking tape strip about a meter long
1 Textbook to put under the board	1 Calculator

Procedure

1. Use a ruler to draw a straight line down the middle of the dry-erase board.

2. Starting at the edge of the board, mark the line in 5-cm intervals.

3. Place the textbook under the board, and secure it with tape so it will not move. The 5-cm marks should be closest to the ground. Place the jingle bell on the ground, in the path of the golf ball.

4. Starting at the first 5-cm interval, align the golf ball with the mark.

5. Let go of the golf ball, but do not push it.

6. Use a ruler to measure the distance the golf ball traveled from the end of the board to its stopping place. Record the noise level (soft, medium, loud) of the jingle bell as the golf ball collided with it.

7. Record this information in the data table on page 2.

8. Repeat the procedure three times at each interval (each interval is 5 cm farther from the previous interval).

9. Find the average distance the golf ball traveled at each interval by adding up the numbers for each trial and dividing that answer by three. You may use a calculator, with your teacher's permission.

Explore 1

Distance Traveled (cm) and Noise Level				
Intervals	Trial 1	Trial 2	Trial 3	Average Distance
5 cm				
10 cm				
15 cm				
20 cm				
25 cm				
30 cm				

1. At which interval did the golf ball travel the farthest? How would you describe the sound created by the jingle bell when the objects collided?

_____

_____

2. How did the ramp's height affect the sound coming from the jingle bell whenthe golf ball was released and the objects collided?

_____

_____

3. Which height do you think led to the moving golf ball having the most energy?

_____

4. Write a sentence or two explaining the relationship between speed and energy.

_____

_____

🔍 Explore 1

Racing for Distance

Claim-Evidence-Reasoning

Use scientific reasoning to explain which ramp interval caused the ball to have the most energy.

Claim:

_____

_____

_____

_____

_____

Evidence:

_____

_____

_____

_____

_____

Reasoning:

_____

_____

_____

_____

_____

Name: _____ Date: _____

 **Explore 2**

Creepy Crawlers

Race Results

Group Member Name	Trial 1 (seconds)	Trial 2 (seconds)	Trial 3 (seconds)

Circle the name of the group member with the fastest time.

1. What did you do to make your climber move faster?

_____

_____

2. What statement can you make about the speed and energy of your climber?

_____

_____

3. What statement can you make regarding speed and energy?

_____

_____

Linking Literacy
Pre-Reading

Rolling Pencils

Before you read: Write a description for each result you got when you pushed the pencils. Then draw a picture to explain your description.

Lightly push your pencil. Describe the result.	Draw an image.

Push your pencil, using more force. Describe the result.	Draw an image.

Linking Literacy
During-Reading

3-2-1 Notes

Complete the table below:

3 **3** Facts about Energy and Speed	
2 **2** Examples of How Energy and Speed Are Related	
1 **1** Question You Still Have about Energy and Speed	

Linking Literacy
Post-Reading

Energy and Speed

Walk Around Paragraph

Write a sentence to answer the question below. At your teacher's signal, move to another student's paper, read his or her sentence, and write another sentence that expands on his or her thought. You will continue this pattern until you and your classmates have written an entire paragraph.

Describe how forces can affect the motion of an object.

Sentence one answers the prompt:

In addition . . .

Also . . .

Finally . . .

📖 Reading Science

A Winning Force

1. The world is always moving and changing. There is motion all around us. On a cool autumn day, the wind causes the leaves on a tree to shake and fall. Ocean waves lift a surfer and push her toward the shore. A baseball flies into the outfield after being hit by a batter. Forces cause objects to change their speed and direction.

2. Objects change direction when a force is applied. When you push a shopping basket, the basket moves in the direction of the force you used. It will continue to move as long as you push it. The greater the applied force, the farther or faster the basket will travel. A faster-moving basket has more energy. Once you stop pushing the basket, it will stop moving. There is no longer a force acting on it to overcome the forces of gravity and friction, which act to hold the basket down in one spot.

3. When you ride a bike, you are changing your motion by **accelerating**. When you push down on the bike pedals, you apply a force that turns the wheels. As you push harder on the pedals, your bike speeds up. This is not the only example of acceleration. When you drop an object, the force of gravity pulls it toward the ground. The force of gravity pulls for as long as the object is in the air. As the object falls farther and farther, it falls faster and faster. It accelerates.

4. An opposing force moves in the opposite direction of another force. It causes the object the forces are acting upon to slow down or stop. Think of a time when you were walking your dog. If your dog tried to chase a cat, the dog was pulling forward. When you pulled on the leash, you were pulling backward. Your pull was an opposing force that caused your dog to slow down or stop. There are also opposing forces in a tennis match. Both players try to keep the ball from going over the back line. They stop the forward movement of the ball by hitting it with their rackets. The swing's force makes the ball change direction and fly back over the net.

5. Think about forces the next time you are playing football, soccer, or tennis with your friends. If you apply a greater force to the ball, it will move faster and farther. Share this with your entire team, and you will be sure to win!

Reading Science

1. Complete the following analogy.

Pedaling a bike is to acceleration as pulling back on a dog's leash is to–

A. energy.

B. gravity.

C. acceleration.

D. deceleration.

2. Complete this sentence with one of the choices below.

The greater the force applied to an object, the farther or _____ the object will move.

A. slower

B. faster

C. lower

D. timer

3. Which of the following is the best example of an opposing force?

A. Pulling on a dog's leash when the dog starts running

B. Kicking a football

C. Pushing bike pedals

D. Pushing a shopping basket at a grocery store

 **Reading Science**

4. Which of the following requires the most force?

    A.   Throwing a paper airplane

    B.   Throwing a bowling ball

    C.   Throwing a basketball

    D.   Throwing a pebble

5. Which of the following is a force of nature?

    A.   A student's friend pushing a shopping cart

    B.   Wind blowing leaves off a tree

    C.   An athlete hitting a baseball with a bat

    D.   An athlete kicking a football into the air

Name: _____ Date: _____

∞ Open-Ended Response

Short Answer:

1. Which will have more energy—a swing being pushed by a small child or a swing being pushed by an adult? Why?

_____

_____

_____

2. Look at the racing data below. Which airplane had the most energy? Which one had the least? Explain how you know. (kph = kilometers per hour)

Airplane	1	2	3
Speed	405 kph	428 kph	417 kph

_____

_____

_____

3. A student has some short and tall ramps and a toy car. She decides to use them to create an investigation. She wants to know which ramp will give the car the most energy. What evidence should she look for? Explain.

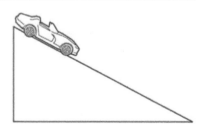

_____

_____

_____

→ Claim-Evidence-Reasoning

Scenario:

Tommy and his dad went to a baseball game. During the first inning, Tommy noticed that when the batter swung the bat very fast and the bat connected with the ball, the ball rocketed off the bat. When the batter bunted (barely tapped) the ball with the bat, the ball fell to the ground. Throughout the game, Tommy noticed there was a relationship between the speed the batters swung their bats and the amount of energy that was transferred to the balls.

Prompt:

Write a scientific explanation for which type of swing had the most energy.

Claim:

_____

_____

_____

_____

Claim-Evidence-Reasoning

Evidence:

_____

_____

_____

_____

_____

_____

Reasoning:

_____

_____

_____

_____

_____

_____

_____

_____

_____

_____

_____

_____

Transfer of Energy in Collision

Name: _____ Date: _____

Graphic Organizer

Crash! Bang! Boom!

Directions

What happens when objects collide? In the first box, write an example of objects colliding. In the second box, write what happens to the objects that collide. Be sure to include in which direction the objects go once they collide.

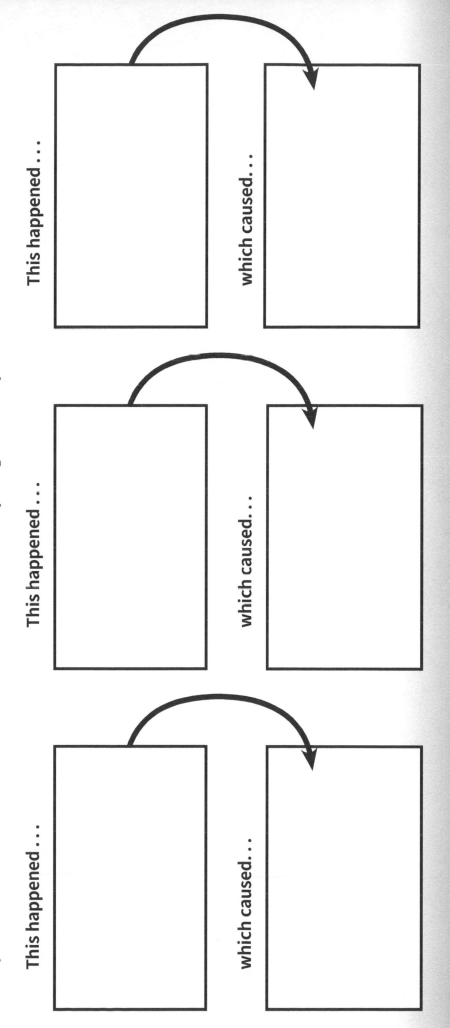

This happened . . .

which caused. . .

This happened . . .

which caused. . .

This happened . . .

which caused. . .

Name: _____ Date: _____

 **Explore 1**

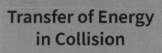
When Cars Collide

Student Data Recording Table

Collision	Before	During	After	Description of Collision
1				
2				
3				

Explore 1

When an object is moving, the object has energy. How was energy transferred in this investigation?

_____

_____

_____

_____

_____

Explore 1

When Cars Collide

Claim-Evidence-Reasoning

Write a scientific explanation for how energy was being transferred from car to car during the collisions.

Claim:

_____

_____

_____

_____

Evidence:

_____

_____

_____

_____

Reasoning:

_____

_____

_____

_____

_____

Explore 2

Let's Bounce

Our Driving Question

How does the weight of a bouncing ball affect objects at rest on a table?

What We Need

1 Basketball

1 Rock, 1–2 cm diameter

1 Golf ball

1 Softball or baseball

1 Metric ruler

10 Pinto beans

1 Pencil

1 Rubber eraser

Procedure

1. Place pinto beans, a pencil, a rubber eraser, and a rock on top of your table.

2. Hold the golf ball 30 centimeters above the tabletop and drop it so it lands close (but not on top of) the items on the table. Use your ruler to measure 30 centimeters.

3. Record what happened to the items on the table in your data table on the next page.

4. Repeat these actions with the baseball or softball and the basketball.

5. Complete three trials for each ball.

Explore 2

Record your data and observations in the table below.

	Trial 1	Trial 2	Trial 3
Golf Ball			
Baseball or Softball			
Basketball			

Why do you think the falling ball made the object move?

_____

_____

_____

Describe another way energy was transferred in the collision.

_____

_____

_____

Name: _____ Date: _____

 **Explore 2**

When Cars Collide
Claim-Evidence-Reasoning

Write a scientific explanation for which ball transferred the least amount of energy to the table.

Claim:

_____

_____

_____

_____

Evidence:

_____

_____

_____

_____

Reasoning:

_____

_____

_____

_____

Explore 3

Collision Machine

The Problem

You have entered a contest to create a "collision machine" for the state fair. The state fair committee shows you a picture of a Rube Goldberg machine to give you an idea of what they are looking for. The committee tells you that in order to win, your machine must have at least four different collisions and must be the most unique and entertaining.

The Challenge

Design and construct a collision machine for the state fair.

Criteria and Constraints

- Your machine must include at least five dominoes, a pendulum to start the chain reaction, a target to hit, and something that makes sound when hit.

- You may use the materials provided or bring materials from home.

- Your machine must fit on top of a student desk.

- Your machine parts must make at least four different collisions and a sound.

- You must first research pendulums, then build your own pendulum, using a 20-cm, 40-cm, or 60- cm string with three washers attached to the end.

Brainstorm and Research

Write down any ideas you have about how you could master the challenge. If you need more information, write down what you need to know and gain permission from your teacher to research the answer.

Explore 3

Design Plan

Use the ideas you wrote down while brainstorming to develop a final design plan. Draw your plan and label the parts. Be sure to list what each part is made of.

Build and Test

Build your design and test it. Does it meet all the criteria and constraints? Use the space below to list what problems you need to fix in your design.

_____

_____

_____

Refine and Redesign

How could you solve the problems you found during testing? Use the space below to draw your new design that should solve the problems.

Explore 3

Retest and Finalize

Build and test your new design. Does it meet all the criteria and constraints? If not, repeat the refine and redesign process. If so, move on to planning your presentation.

Presentation Plan

Use the space below to plan how you will present your final product. Be sure to include who will speak and what you want to say. Your presentation should include the scientific ideas used to solve this design challenge.

Linking Literacy
Pre-Reading

Think About It

Directions: Think of all the types of energy that you know about and write them on the lightning bolts.

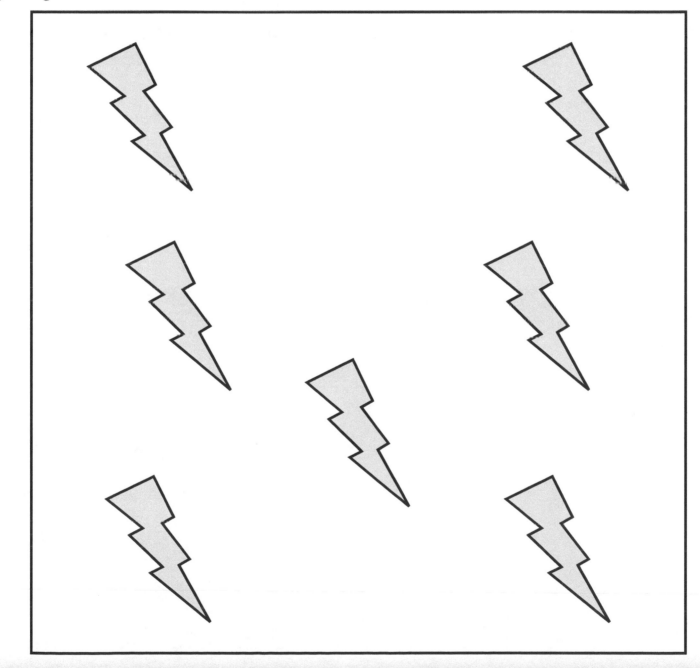

Linking Literacy
During-Reading

Guided Notes

While you read: Use the information from the text to complete the statements below.

1. When two objects collide, they can create _____ and _____ energy.

2. When you knock on a door, your hand _____ energy to the door. The energy then passes through the door to the _____ on the other side. The waves that pass through the air are what we _____ as a knock.

3. When you clap your hands one time or twelve times, as instructed in the reading, energy is transferred from the collision of your moving hands and creates _____ and _____.

4. When energy gets transferred in a collision, it can cause the _____ of the objects to change.

In the space below, record any other information you learned from the reading.

_____

_____

_____

_____

_____

_____

_____

_____

Name: _____   Date: _____

Linking Literacy
Post-Reading

Four-Corner Summary

After you read: Copy the following onto a note card. Using your notes from the text, write four facts about the center topic. Then turn each fact into a sentence, forming a paragraph on the back of the note card.

FACT

FACT

Energy Is Transferred in a Collision

FACT

FACT

Name: _____ Date: _____

Reading Science

Crater Creation

1. Have you ever looked up at the Moon at night? What did you see? At times, the Moon can look like a smooth, glowing ball. But nothing could be further from the truth.

2. The Moon is covered with craters. Craters are bowl-shaped holes. They are formed when objects from space hit the Moon. If these same objects were to head toward Earth, they would probably burn up when they hit Earth's atmosphere, or they would get slowed down by our atmosphere. But the Moon has no atmosphere. So, there is nothing to stop them from hitting its surface.

3. Have you ever seen a rock falling into a puddle of water? That's what it looks like when a meteoroid, or piece of rock, hits the surface of the Moon. It throws up dust and dirt, just like a rock would splash water into the air. The meteoroid breaks up into pieces. It leaves a ring on the surface. The dust and dirt that splash out even create bright lines that look like rays.

4. You can tell a lot by looking at these craters. If a large rock hits the Moon's surface, it makes a big ring. Smaller rocks make smaller rings. A deep crater means that the rock that hit the Moon's surface was moving very fast, while a smaller crater means that it was moving slower.

5. One crater that amazes scientists is named Tycho. Tycho is one of the only craters where the bright lines coming out of the crater can be seen clearly. These rays can be seen because Tycho is pretty young for a large crater. It's only 108 million years old! That might seem old to you. But some of the craters are over one billion years old!

6. The patterns found on the surface of the Moon tell scientists a lot of details. The information tells them about dust particles and other objects that were floating in space millions of years ago. Scientists can even learn about what happened on the Moon before people were on Earth. All this is possible because of the patterns created from the force of rocks hitting the Moon's surface.

7. Next time you look at the Moon, think about all the craters. Some of them are so big that you can even see them with your own eyes!

1. The author probably wrote this passage to–

   A. persuade the reader to study the Moon.

   B. entertain the reader with stories about the Moon.

   C. inform the reader about what scientists can learn from craters on the Moon.

   D. explain how to use information about craters to calculate how fast meteoroids were traveling when they hit the Moon.

2. Scientists measured the depth of four craters. Their data is in the table below. Assuming all meteoroids were the same size and mass, which crater was caused by a meteoroid moving at the fastest speed?

   A. Crater A

   B. Crater B

   C. Crater C

   D. Crater D

Crater A	5 m
Crater B	25 m
Crater C	4 m
Crater D	27 m

3. Another good title for this passage would be–

   A. "Learning from the Moon's Craters."

   B. "Scientists on the Moon."

   C. "Tycho the Crater."

   D. "Objects in Space."

Reading Science

4. Scientists found two crater rings, one on top of the other. They could tell–

    A. how fast the meteoroids that formed the craters were traveling.

    B. the crater on the bottom was older.

    C. the shape of the meteoroid.

    D. what the crater should be named.

5. Why aren't there as many craters on Earth as there are on the Moon?

    A. People are able to keep the meteoroids from hitting Earth.

    B. Meteoroids never come near Earth.

    C. Earth's atmosphere causes most meteoroids to burn up.

    D. People fill in the craters that are formed.

∞ **Open-Ended Response**

1. What will happen to the ball when the soccer player kicks it?

_____

_____

_____

2. Have you ever bumped into someone? Describe the transfer of energy that happened and how it affected the motion of you and the other person.

_____

_____

_____

3. Look at the picture provided. Observe the bowling ball as it collides with the pins. How are the pins changing position? How is energy being transferred?

_____

_____

_____

Claim-Evidence-Reasoning

Scenario:

The class took a field trip to a bowling alley. They noticed several energy transfers as they bowled.

Prompt:

Write a scientific explanation for what happens when the bowling ball makes contact with the pins.

Claim:

_____

_____

_____

_____

_____

_____

_____

Claim-Evidence-Reasoning

Evidence:

_____

_____

_____

_____

_____

Reasoning:

_____

_____

_____

_____

_____

_____

_____

_____

_____

California Instructional Segment
Mission Log

Mission Log

Anchoring Phenomena

How do we get electricity and fuel to run and power electronic devices using renewable resources?

Mission Briefing

You work for a company that makes camping equipment. They have asked you to design a spinning system that can attach to a generator and power a hot plate. The system must use a renewable resource and not pollute the environment.

- What renewable resource will your system use that is available in the forest?

- How can the system connect to the generator and the hot plate?

California Instructional Segment
Mission Log

Class Mission Log

Information Gained

Transfer of Energy in Collision

Think back to what you learned before to answer the following question:

How is energy transferred when objects collide?

_____

_____

_____

Using Stored Energy

What do a battery and food have in common?

_____

_____

_____

Connection to Mission

Transfer of Energy in Collision

Think back to what you learned before to answer the following question:

How does the energy get transferred from the moving system to the hot plate?

_____

_____

_____

Using Stored Energy

Brainstorm ways that you could convert mechanical energy into heat energy.

_____

_____

_____

California Instructional Segment

Mission Log

Mission Log

Information Gained

Renewable and Nonrenewable Resources

How does human use of natural resources affect the environment?

_____

_____

_____

Environmental Changes and Effects

What basic parts does a circuit need?

_____

_____

_____

Connection to Mission

Renewable and Nonrenewable Resources

What natural resources could your system use? How?

_____

_____

_____

Environmental Changes and Effects

What type of energy is being converted into electrical energy to power the hot plate?

_____

_____

_____

California Instructional Segment

Action Plan

Action Plan

Design a system that can spin using a renewable resource to create electricity and power a hot plate for use on a camping trip.

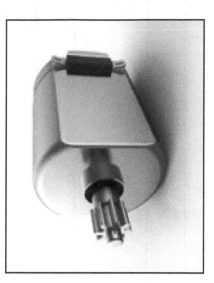

Here's what we know:

- The system needs a hole in the center so it can attach to the generator.

- You cannot touch the system to make it spin.

- The renewable resource cannot pollute the environment or disturb the wildlife

California Instructional Segment

Action Plan

Take Action

What materials will your system use?

_____

_____

_____

Why did you choose these materials?

_____

_____

_____

What natural resource will make your system spin?

_____

_____

_____

Why did you choose that natural resource?

_____

_____

_____

California Instructional Segment

Action Plan

Take Action

Draw your system. Use arrows to show the direction of the spin.

California Instructional Segment

Action Plan

Take Action

Draw your design attached to the generator and complete a circuit to connect the generator to the hot plate.

Using Stored Energy

Explore 1

More Energy Please!

Our Driving Question

How can stored energy be converted into forms for practical use?

What We Need

Part I:

1 Foam ball

5 Plastic spoons

1 Skewer

1 Bottle of water

Part II:

1 AAA battery

1 C battery

1 9 V battery

1 Miniature lightbulb

2 Insulated copper wires with wire ends exposed

Explore 1

Procedure

Part I: Build a Water Turbine

1. Build your model.

   a. Stick a pencil through the center of the foam ball. You will need to do this so the skewer fits through the hole and the ball can spin freely around the skewer.

   b. Break the handles off each spoon. BE CAREFUL! Broken edges can be sharp.

   c. Stick the handle part into the ball in a line around the ball so that the spoons are perpendicular to the skewer. Be sure they are facing the same direction and are evenly spread out.

   d. Take the spoons out and let your teacher fill each hole with a small amount of hot glue. Stick the spoons back into the holes. This will prevent them from falling out during the activity.

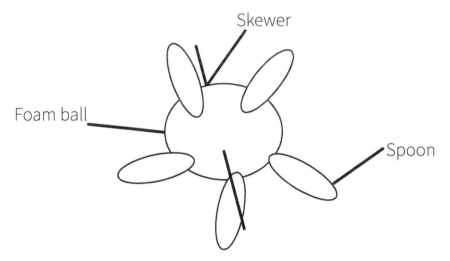

2. Go outside for the activity.

3. One group member should hold either end of the skewer.

4. Another group member should hold the water bottle a few inches directly above the turbine and pour half the water onto the turbine.

5. Record your observations on the next page.

6. Repeat steps 3–4, but this time, hold the water bottle as high above the turbine as you can. Pour half the water onto the turbine.

7. Record your observations on on the next pages and answer the reflection questions.

Explore 1

Part II: Comparing Batteries

1. You should have three different-sized batteries, copper wires, and a miniature lightbulb.

2. Start with the smallest battery and create a circuit. Your goal is to make the lightbulb light up.

3. Draw your circuit in the table and record your observations.

4. Use the medium-sized battery and create a circuit. Your goal is to make the lightbulb light up.

5. Draw your circuit in the table and record your observations.

6. Use the largest battery and create a circuit. Your goal is to make the lightbulb light up.

7. Draw your circuit in the table and record your observations.

8. Answer the reflection questions.

Explore 1

Part I: Build a Water Turbine

Record your observations in the boxes below. Describe the speed of the turbine when water was poured from different distances above it.

Water Poured a Few Inches above Turbine	Water Poured High above Turbine

1. When did the turbine spin the fastest?

_____

2. At which distance above the turbine do you think there was more stored energy?

_____

3. What type of energy is released from the stored energy?

_____

_____

4. What are water turbines used for in everyday life?

_____

_____

5. Draw a waterfall. Place an *X* on the best location to put the turbine to get the most mechanical energy out of the waterfall. Explain why you chose the location.

_____

_____

Explore 1

Part II: Comparing Batteries

Draw each circuit in the boxes below.

Battery	Drawing of Circuit
AAA	
C	
9 V	

Explore 1

Part II: Reflection Questions

1. Which battery has the most stored energy?

_____

2. Which battery has the least stored energy?

_____

3. What type of energy was produced when the stored energy in each battery was released?

_____

4. Which battery caused the lightbulb to appear the brightest?

_____

5. What is the relationship between the amount of stored energy and the amount of energy released?

_____

_____

_____

6. Why do we use different-sized batteries for different things in everyday life?

_____

_____

_____

_____

Explore 2

History of Transportation

For each type of transportation, write where energy is stored. Then cut out the energy cards and place them in the *Type of Stored Energy* and *Comes from and Used For* columns. Check with your teacher before gluing them down. Finally, write the types of energy that the stored energy produces.

Transportation	Place Energy Is Stored	Type of Stored Energy	Comes from and Used For	Type of Energy Produced
Horse and carriage				
Gas-powered car				
Electric car				
Steam engine				
Dogsled				
Wheelbarrow				

Why is it necessary for forms of transportation to have a way to store energy?

_____

_____

_____

_____

Explore 2

History of Transportation
Energy Cards

Stored Energy Type	Comes from and Used For
Chemical	Burning coal; making steam and pulling the cars
Chemical	Eating food; moving muscles
Chemical	Gasoline being burned; turning the tires
Chemical	Eating food; moving muscles
Chemical	Eating food; moving muscles
Chemical	Chemicals reacting; turning the tires

🔍 Explore 2

History of Transportation
Claim-Evidence-Reasoning

Write a scientific explanation about what can happen to stored energy.

Claim:

_____

_____

_____

Evidence:

_____

_____

_____

_____

_____

_____

Reasoning:

_____

_____

_____

_____

_____

_____

Reading Science

A Wild Weather Day

1. It was a hot and humid day in Central Oklahoma. Chloe and her friend, Sophie, were outside playing on the Slip'N' Slide. It was helping them stay cool.

2. "This is so much better! It is so hot!" said Chloe. She ran and belly flopped on the slide.

3. "Watch how fast I slide!" yelled Sophie as she went splashing through the water.

4. The girls continued to play for most of the afternoon. They began getting tired. They stopped to rest and have a snack so they could continue sliding. Before long, they noticed the Sun was beginning to disappear. Dark clouds were filling the sky in the distance. In school, Sophie and Chloe had learned that dark clouds mean it is time to check the weather forecast.

5. Chloe grabbed her towel. She ran inside to grab her hand-crank radio so she could listen to the weather. Chloe had charged it the week before. She charged it by plugging it into the wall. Chloe's weather radio had saved energy in its battery. Chloe turned the crank many times. The radio turned on. It changed the stored electrical energy to sound energy. Chloe and Sophie listened **intently** to the radio. They learned there was a tornado watch. Both girls quickly cleaned up the Slip'N Slide. They took it to the garage.

6. Once inside, Chloe plugged in her radio. Chloe knew her radio would need to be fully charged. They would use it if the lights were to go out. She turned on the TV. The light from the TV lit the dark room. The girls turned on the local news station. They could see the approaching storm on the radar. The meteorologist predicted the storm was heading toward them.

7. "We better gather some snacks, a flashlight, my cell phone, Band-Aids, and blankets," said Sophie. The girls moved around the house, quickly putting together their emergency kit. The phone rang. It was Chloe's mom.

8. "Okay, Mom. We are getting our things now and going to the basement," said Chloe. She could feel butterflies in her stomach. She knew Oklahoma storms could be **vicious**.

9. "I love you, Mom," cried Chloe as she hung up the phone.

10. Sophie had gathered the rest of the supplies. The girls could hear the wind picking up. The TV went dark. There was no more light shining in the room.

11. "A power line must be down! The electricity has been cut off!!" cried Sophie. The winds outside began gusting stronger.

12. "Let's get to the basement!" shouted Chloe.

13. Chloe placed the batteries into the flashlight. The batteries soon changed their stored chemical energy into electrical energy, which the flashlight converted into light energy. The light guided the girls to the basement. When the girls reached the basement, they went to the middle bathroom to protect themselves from any windows or possible flying debris. Chloe cranked the radio. The movement of the handle once again converted the stored energy in the battery to electrical energy and, eventually, to sound energy.

14. "All citizens should seek shelter," announced the man on the radio. "A tornado is passing through and is moving at 30 mph. Wind gusts up to 150 mph are possible. The National Weather Service has issued a tornado warning for Warren County. All citizens should take shelter now."

15. The girls huddled close. They held their flashlights and sang "Twinkle, Twinkle, Little Star" to help calm their fears. The wind howled. The windows rattled. They heard rain and debris hitting the windows.

16. Ten minutes later, the winds calmed. All that could be heard was the steady sound of rain. Chloe and Sophie cranked the weather radio.

17. "Citizens of Warren County are out of the danger zone. You may now come out of shelter. Be careful of any fallen debris," said the man on the radio.

Reading Science

18. Chloe and Sophie quickly grabbed the phone to call their parents. They were so excited to be safe and sound. They went upstairs. They saw fallen trees and signs. They noticed a broken window in the kitchen. The wind was blowing through it.

19. "We did it!" Sophie cried. She wrapped her arms around Chloe. Within minutes, the TV came back on.

20. "They must have fixed the power line," said Chloe.

21. "Thank goodness," sighed Sophie.

22. As they curled up on the couch to watch the news about the storm, they thought about their wild-weather day. They could not wait until their parents returned home so they could share their brave stories about the stormy day.

Reading Science

1. What words does the author use to convey a distressed mood?

    A. "Thank goodness," sighed Sophie.

    B. Chloe knew her radio would need to be fully charged.

    C. "Let's get to the basement!" shouted Chloe.

    D. "This is much better! It is so hot!"

2. The reader can tell–

    A. The girls love storms.

    B. The girls are home alone for the first time during a storm.

    C. The radio is operated by electrical energy.

    D. The storm destroyed the community.

3. The phrase *butterflies in her stomach* tells the reader–

    A. Chloe was content.

    B. Chloe was determined.

    C. Chloe was concerned

    D. Chloe was courageous.

Reading Science

4. What evidence helps the reader know what the word *intently* means?

   A. *The meteorologist predicted the storm was heading toward them.*

   B. *In school, Sophie and Chloe had learned that dark clouds mean it is time to check the weather forecast.*

   C. *Chloe grabbed her towel. She ran inside to grab her hand-crank radio. . .*

   D. *They learned there was a tornado watch.*

5. What is a synonym for the word *vicious*?

   A. Pure

   B. Monstrous

   C. Respectable

   D. Coarse

6. If the author had wanted to give the reader an example of debris, which of the following words could she or he have used?

   A. Trash, junk, and tree limbs

   B. Dogs, cats, and ants

   C. Street signs, sea turtles, and T-shirts

   D. Sink, mug, and fork

Reading Science

7. Which of the following pieces of evidence helps the reader know energy is not created but, instead, changes forms?

   A. *They stopped to rest and have a snack so they could continue sliding.*

   B. *"They must have fixed the power line."*

   C. *Ten minutes later, the winds calmed. All that could be heard was the steady sound of rain.*

   D. *Chloe turned the crank several times. The radio turned on.*

8. The sentence, *"We did it!" Sophie cried as she wrapped her arms around Chloe*, tells the reader–

   A. Sophie was very depressed.

   B. Sophie was very relieved.

   C. Sophie was very jovial.

   D. Sophie was very distraught.

Name: _____ Date: _____

∞ Open-Ended Response

1. Describe how a flashlight works. What makes the flashlight produce light?

_____

_____

_____

_____

2. Your sister's favorite toy is a doll that moves and talks. The doll uses batteries to supply it with the energy to complete these tasks. What would happen if the stored energy in the batteries ran out?

_____

_____

_____

_____

3. How would you explain to a friend how a car works? Where does it get energy to run? What types of energy transformations need to happen to make the car move?

_____

_____

_____

_____

Claim-Evidence-Reasoning

Using Stored Energy

Scenario:

Annalise got a new toy for her birthday! It was a metal toy monkey with moveable arms holding cymbals. The package said the toy could light up and that it would hit the cymbals together to make noise when it is turned on. Annalise excitedly pulled it out of the package and turned it on. Nothing happened. Annalise told her mom that her toy was not working. Her mom opened the bottom, put batteries inside, and gave it back to Annalise. She turned it on again and it worked! The lights started flashing and the cymbals started clanking!

Prompt:

Use scientific reasoning to explain why Annalise's mom put batteries in the toy.

Claim:

_____

_____

_____

_____

_____

_____

_____

_____

Claim-Evidence-Reasoning

Evidence:

_____

_____

_____

_____

_____

_____

Reasoning:

_____

_____

_____

_____

_____

_____

_____

_____

_____

_____

_____

Renewable and Nonrenewable Resources

Name: _____ Date: _____

Graphic Organizer

Using Renewable Resources

Directions

There are many ways to use renewable resources. In the web below, describe ways we can use renewable resources.

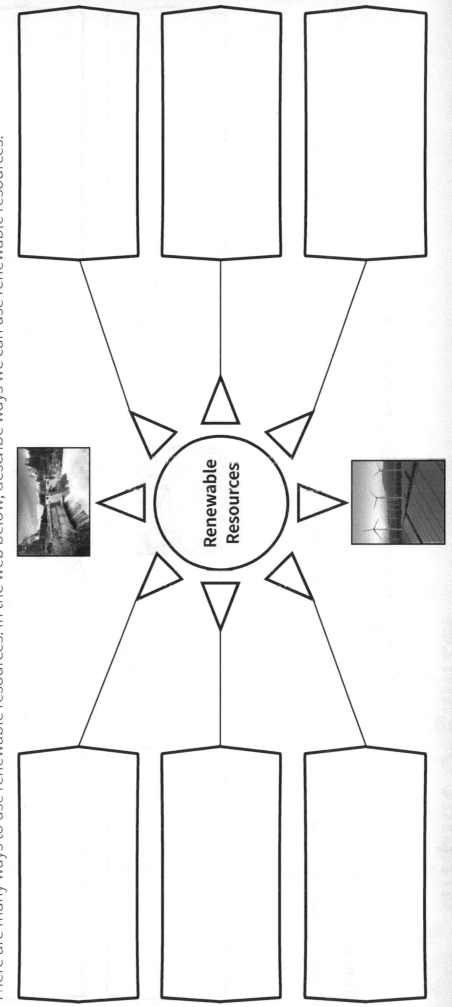

![Graphic Organizer icon] **Graphic Organizer**

Using Nonrenewable Resources

Directions

Nonrenewable resources are used in many ways. In the web below, describe ways we use nonrenewable resources.

Nonrenewable Resources

Name: _____ Date: _____

 **Explore 1**

How Can We Classify Natural Resources?

Directions

- Separate the cards by type. You should have six RESOURCES stacks and one EVENT stack.

- Turn the event cards facedown.

- Take turns drawing cards and follow the directions on the card.

- Nonrenewable resource cards should be moved to the side and cannot be used again.

- Renewable resource cards should be put back into the stack after one minute. Use a stopwatch or timer to help with this. (This is like the resources being replaced in a lifetime.)

- Continue to play the game until you are out of all event cards.

- Complete your Student Journal.

1. In the game, what were the renewable resources?

_____

_____

2. What does *renewable* mean?

_____

_____

3. In the game, what were the nonrenewable resources?

_____

_____

4. What does *nonrenewable* mean?

_____

_____

Explore 1

5.

Draw Three Renewable Resources	Draw Three Nonrenewable Resources

6. Which resources were used to make fuel?

_____

_____

7. Where do all these resources come from?

_____

_____

8. Explain why renewable and nonrenewable resources are important to humans.

_____

_____

Explore 2

Effects of Energy Skit

Record the environmental effects of the energy sources in the table below.

Environmental Effects of Natural Energy Resources
Solar Energy
Hydroelectric Energy
Fossil Fuels
Wind Energy

🔍 Explore 2

Which energy source caused the least harm?

_____

_____

_____

_____

How was the wildlife affected by the energy resources?

_____

_____

_____

_____

How were humans affected by the energy resources?

_____

_____

_____

_____

Name: _____ Date: _____

 **Explore 2**

Effects of Energy Skit
Claim-Evidence-Reasoning

Write a scientific explanation for the relationship between the use of natural energy resources and the effect they have on the environment.

Claim:

_____

_____

_____

Evidence:

_____

_____

_____

_____

_____

Reasoning:

_____

_____

_____

_____

Name: _____ Date: _____

Explore 3

Renewable and Nonrenewable Resources

Introduction

McCally is a town with a problem. Its citizens would like to find a different energy source so they can get away from burning fossil fuels. The area is very dry except for one big river, and the area has lots of open areas. A lot of birds and animals migrate through the area twice a year. It is also a major manufacturer of video games. Help McCally find a different energy source.

What we will research:

_____

_____

We need to look for answers to following questions:

a. Question 1?

_____

_____

b. Question 2?

_____

_____

c. Question 3?

_____

_____

Explore 3

Organize

Use this space to organize the information you gathered.

Record your sources below.

Source Used	Type of Source	Author	Is it Credible?

Explore 3

Present

Think about how you will present what you learned to the class. Use the table below to plan and organize what you learned to create your presentation.

How Will You Introduce Your Topic?	
Main Point 1 (What was the answer to your first question?)	
Main Point 2 (What was the answer to your second question?)	
Main Point 3 (What was the answer to your third question?)	
Summarize Your Main Points to End Your Presentation.	

Present your presentation to the class! Take some time to listen to feedback from your teacher and classmates. Discuss in your group what you did well and how you could have done better.

Name: _____ Date: _____

Linking Literacy
Pre-Reading

Resources Quick Write

Directions: Write down everything you know about renewable and nonrenewable resources in the time allowed.

_____

_____

_____

_____

_____

_____

_____

_____

_____

_____

_____

_____

_____

_____

_____

_____

_____

_____

_____

_____

Name: _____ Date: _____

Linking Literacy
During-Reading

Classifying Examples of Resources

Directions: While reading, choose a resource and write it in the first column. Illustrate it in the second column and classify it as an **R** (renewable) or **NR** (nonrenewable) resource by putting an X in the correct column.

Resources	Illustration	R	NR

Name: _____ Date: _____

Linking Literacy
Post-Reading

Walk Around Paragraph

Write a sentence that answers the prompt. On your teacher's signal, move to another student's paper, read his or her sentence, and write a sentence elaborating on his or her thought. The process will continue until you have written an entire paragraph.

Choose a renewable resource and explain how its uses affect the environment.

Sentence one answers the prompt:

In addition . . .

Also . . .

Finally . . .

Name: _____   Date: _____

📖 Reading Science

The Poster Contest

1. One day, after lunch, Miss Simpson made an announcement to her class.

2. "Class," she said, "we are going to participate in a poster contest. We are going to create posters that encourage kids to use resources wisely."

3. "What does that mean?" asked John.

4. Miss Simpson replied, "Earth provides us with the numerous resources we need to survive. Earth provides the following natural resources: air, plants, water, animals, and minerals. Humans cannot produce these resources themselves, but instead, they rely on Earth to provide them."

5. "Why do we have to use them wisely?" asked Amir.

6. "Well," Miss Simpson went on, "some resources are renewable, which means we can use them again and again." Holding up a piece of notebook paper, Miss Simpson continued. "For example, this paper is made from trees. When trees are cut down to make products, such as paper, they can be regrown. However, it takes a long time for a new tree to grow and mature. We can also replace dirty water with clean water and clean the air after it has been polluted, but these also take a long time. These are just a couple of the reasons we need to take care of our renewable resources."

7. "What about things that cannot be renewed?" asked Addison. "My dad says there is only so much oil in the world, so we have to **conserve**, or not use so much of it."

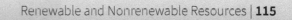

8. "That is correct, Addy," said Miss Simpson. "Besides oil, there are nonrenewable resources such as coal and natural gas, also known as fossil fuels. Once we use all the available nonrenewable resources, that will be it. We will no longer have more to take their places. It took the planet millions of years to create these resources, and we are using them so quickly that current supplies will be depleted if we continue to consume them at the rate we are now. You kids are so smart. I know you will want to help spread the word about using resources wisely."

9. "I think this poster contest sounds like a great idea!" said Amir. "I don't want us to run out of resources!"

10. Miss Simpson passed out crayons, paper, and markers to the kids. They immediately began working on their posters. They drew pictures and wrote messages to encourage others to use resources wisely for a better Earth.

11. On their posters, the students wrote various slogans, such as "Please Recycle!" and "Walk to Save Gas." In addition, Miss Simpson gave ideas, such as, "Turn Off the Water When You Brush Your Teeth!" and "Reuse Plastic Bottles."

12. After the class finished the posters for the contest, Miss Simpson asked the kids to make some additional posters to put around the school, so all the other students could learn about using resources wisely.

13. The kids hung their posters with pride. They felt like they had done something good for their school as well as for their planet. Miss Simpson was proud of them, too, and treated all the kids to some cupcakes that she had made.

Reading Science

1. What is the story mainly about?

    A.   Students learning about resources and the importance of using them wisely

    B.   Students entering a poster contest

    C.   Miss Simpson being a kind and knowledgeable teacher

    D.   Students decorating their school with posters

2. Which of these is most likely to happen the next day at school?

    A.   Miss Simpson will teach a math lesson.

    B.   Amir, John, and Addison will throw away paper and plastic bottles.

    C.   Other students at school will see the posters and recycle.

    D.   The principal will get upset because the kids put up posters without permission.

3. What does the author mean by the word **_conserve_** (seventh paragraph)?

    A.   Save

    B.   Convince

    C.   Use

    D.   Waste

Reading Science

4. Complete this analogy: Trees are to renewable as _____ is to nonrenewable.

    A.   water

    B.   oil

    C.   corn

    D.   money

5. Which of these statements from the passage is Miss Simpson's opinion?

    A.   "We are going to participate in a poster contest."

    B.   "When trees are cut down to make products, such as paper, they can be regrown."

    C.   "Besides oil, there are nonrenewable resources such as coal and natural gas, also known as fossil fuels."

    D.   "You kids are so smart. I know you will want to help spread the word about using resources wisely."

Name: _____ Date: _____

∞ Open-Ended Response

1. Why are coal, oil, and natural gas considered nonrenewable resources?

_____

_____

_____

_____

2. Dams help us use the power of moving water to create electricity. How is using this type of renewable energy helpful to the environment? How is it harmful?

_____

_____

_____

_____

3. What are some ways your family uses energy in your home? Describe how your family could conserve energy.

_____

_____

_____

_____

Claim-Evidence-Reasoning

Renewable and Nonrenewable Resources

Scenario:

The pie chart below shows the energy sources used in 2010.

External Data:

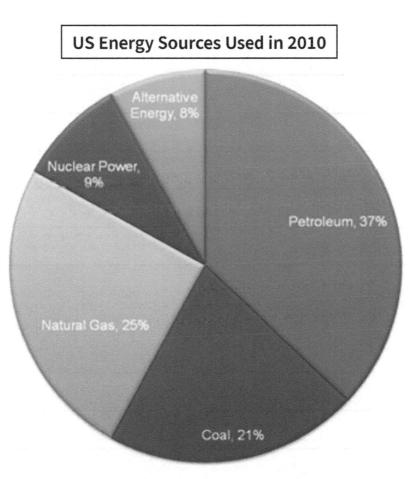

US Energy Sources Used in 2010

Alternative Energy, 8%

Nuclear Power, 9%

Petroleum, 37%

Natural Gas, 25%

Coal, 21%

Prompt:

Write a scientific explanation that describes whether the United States used more renewable or nonrenewable energy resources in 2010.

Claim-Evidence-Reasoning

Claim:

_____

_____

_____

_____

Evidence:

_____

_____

_____

_____

_____

_____

Reasoning:

_____

_____

_____

_____

_____

_____

_____

Energy Transfer
and Electric Currents

Name: _____ Date: _____

Graphic Organizer

The Transfer of Energy

Directions

Use what you have learned about electrical energy to fill in the boxes.

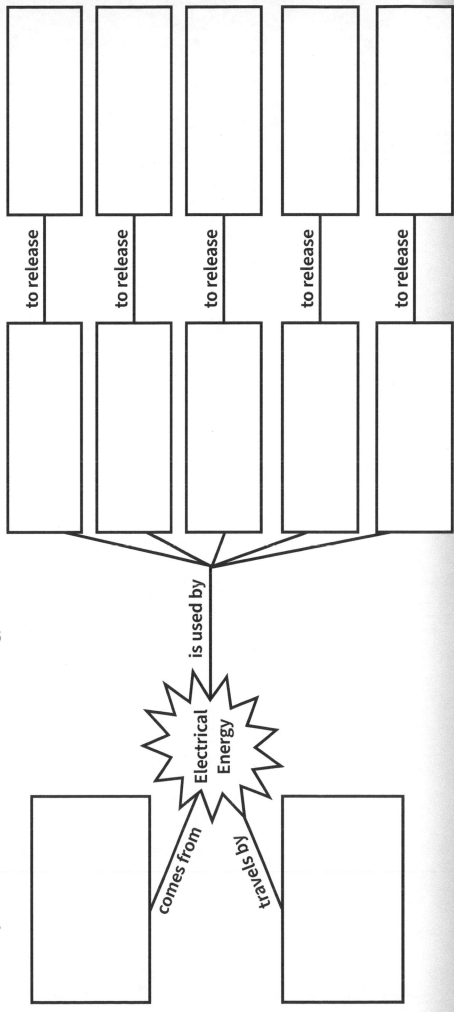

Name: _____ Date: _____

🪝 Hook

Energy in Everyday Objects

Directions: Cut out the pictures on the next page. Decide what types of energy each object gives off. Discuss your reasoning with a partner. Glue each picture in the box with the type of energy it gives off.

Light Energy	Sound Energy
Heat Energy	**Mechanical Energy**

Hook

Name: _____   Date: _____

 **Explore 1**

What's the Buzz?

Student Data Recording Table

Successful Arrangement Diagram (include labels)	Description and Observations	Forms of Energy Observed

Write down any additional questions you might have about electricity, electric currents, and energy transfer.

_____

_____

_____

🔍 Explore 1

What's the Buzz?
Claim-Evidence-Reasoning

Write a scientific explanation for how energy was being transferred in the circuit.

Claim:

_____

_____

_____

Evidence:

_____

_____

_____

Reasoning:

_____

_____

_____

_____

_____

_____

_____

Explore 2

All the Bells and Whistles

The Problem

Ms. Keen's class has been learning about converting stored electrical energy into different forms of energy. The class is working on a fund-raiser booth for their school's fall festival. They want it to attract a lot of attention so they can make a lot of money for their school.

The Challenge

Design a booth that will draw the crowd's attention by including as many examples as possible of electrical energy being transferred to other forms of energy.

Criteria and Constraints

- You must show electrical energy being converted into at least three other forms of energy.
- Your design must show your source of energy and how it is connected to the booth.
- Your design must also show how you plan on controlling the energy (e.g., turning it on and off).
- Your design should be clearly drawn, with all parts labeled.

Brainstorm and Research

Write down any ideas you have about how you could master the challenge. If you need more information, write down what you need to know, and gain permission from your teacher to research the answer.

Explore 2

Design Plan

Use the ideas you wrote down while brainstorming to develop a final design plan. Draw your plan and label the parts. Be sure to list what each part is made of.

Refine and Redesign

Does your design meet all the criteria and constraints? Use the space below to list what problems you need to fix in your design.

_____

_____

_____

_____

Use the space below to draw your new design that should solve the problems.

Explore 2

Retest and Finalize

Look at your design again. Does it meet all the criteria and constraints? If not, repeat the refine and redesign process. If so, move on to planning your presentation.

Presentation Plan

Use the space below to plan how you will present your final product. Be sure to include who will speak and what you want to say. Your presentation should include the scientific ideas used to solve this design challenge.

Write down any additional questions you might have about electricity, electric currents, and energy transfer.

_____

_____

_____

Name: _____ Date: _____

 **Explore 3**

My Energy Transfer Investigation

Plan It!

Our questions: (Reminder: make sure you choose a question that is testable!)

Our ideas for answering our question:

Remember, you can do any of the following.

- Make an observation (What do I see, hear, feel, smell, or taste?)

- Make a model

- Take a survey (I can ask my family and friends a question.)

- Measure and collect data

- Design an experiment

What materials will we need?

What procedure will we follow?

Explore 3

Test It!

Data and observations:

 **Explore 3**

Wrap It Up!

Rewrite your original question:

Write a **claim** that answers your question.

What **evidence** did you gather that supports your claim?

Linking Literacy
Pre- and During-Reading

Definition Continuum

Before you read: Select words from the text. Define the words based on what you think the words mean. Next, add or change the meaning of the words based on the context clues from reading the passage.

Word	Before Reading	During Reading

Linking Literacy
Post-Reading

Draw and Explain

Directions: Students in Mrs. Smith's fourth-grade class were given wires, a battery, a lightbulb, and a buzzer and were asked to make complete circuits. In the space below, draw and label four different circuits the students could make using these materials.

Example 1	Example 2
Example 3	Example 4

In the space below, explain what makes a circuit work.

_____

_____

_____

Reading Science

Two Kinds of Current

1. Look around you, and name five things that use electrical energy. What are they?

2. Many things use electricity, but not all electricity is the same. There are two very different kinds of electricity.

Direct Current

3. The first kind of electricity is called *direct current*, or *DC*. It is called *direct* because it flows from the energy source to the device that uses it. Devices that use batteries get their energy from direct current. They are powered by this kind of electricity. Flashlights and cameras are examples of devices that use direct electric current.

4. A device that uses DC energy has a power source with a positive side and a negative side. Look at a battery closely. You will find that it has a positive and negative side, too. When putting batteries into a flashlight, you have to be careful to match the sides correctly, or else the flashlight will not work.

Alternating Current

5. The other kind of electricity is called *alternating current*, or *AC*. Power plants produce this type of electricity. It is carried by large power lines from the plant to your home. When you plug a TV, a lamp, or a hair dryer into a wall socket, you are using this type of electricity.

6. AC energy cannot go right into TVs and lamps because it is too powerful. It first needs to pass through a transformer. A transformer breaks the electricity down into smaller parts. The transformer sends just the right amount of energy to your home. This prevents your alarm clock from burning up!

7. Now, look around you once again. Can you tell which things use DC electricity and which use AC electricity?

Reading Science

1. The author organized this passage by–

    A.   contrasting DC and AC currents.

    B.   describing the sequence of how power gets to the reader's home.

    C.   explaining the many uses of electricity.

    D.   telling the reader the steps to create a circuit.

2. Which of these household items is powered by alternating current?

    A.   A flashlight

    B.   A remote control

    C.   A hair dryer

    D.   A handheld video game

3. *A transformer breaks the electricity down into smaller parts. The transformer sends just the right amount of energy to your home.* (sixth paragraph)

     Why would a device start burning without the transformer?

    A.   It would not work, so people might throw it in the fireplace.

    B.   The current would be so powerful that it would cause the device to catch on fire.

    C.   A person would not be able to tell which way to plug in the device, so there would be a spark on the wire.

    D.   The battery would explode.

Reading Science

4. What should go in the empty box?

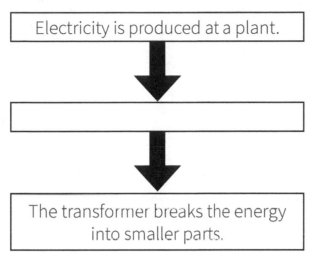

Electricity is produced at a plant.

The transformer breaks the energy into smaller parts.

- **A.** The energy is stored in a battery.
- **B.** A student plugs in their toaster to use energy.
- **C.** Wind, coal, water, or nuclear plants generate electricity.
- **D.** The electricity travels through power lines.

5. Which of the following statements is true of DC and AC currents?

- **A.** They have positive and negative sides.
- **B.** They provide power to devices when they are plugged into a wall socket.
- **C.** They are useful in homes.
- **D.** They would not work without a transformer.

Name: _____ Date: _____

∞ Open-Ended Response

1. Observe the fan. Explain how energy moves within the fan when it is on.

_____

_____

_____

_____

2. Think about your favorite indoor activity. Discuss how circuits are involved with this activity. You could include anything from turning on a light in a room to plugging in a certain device. Be creative and explain how circuits help you conduct the chosen activity.

_____

_____

_____

_____

3. Think about items in your house that use electricity. Describe what happens when you turn the each object on and off. Why does this happen?

_____

_____

_____

_____

Claim-Evidence-Reasoning

Scenario:

One morning before school, Lea decided to prepare some toast. Her toast popped up as the toaster made a "ding!" sound, and the glowing orange coils of the toaster caught her eye. As she buttered her toast, she wondered where the energy in her toaster came from. Her town's main electrical source is a local wind turbine farm. The wind turbines turn and cause the generator to spin and create electricity. This electrical energy is then sent to the town's homes through power lines. Look at the diagram below to see how the energy travels from the wind turbines to an appliance.

External Data:

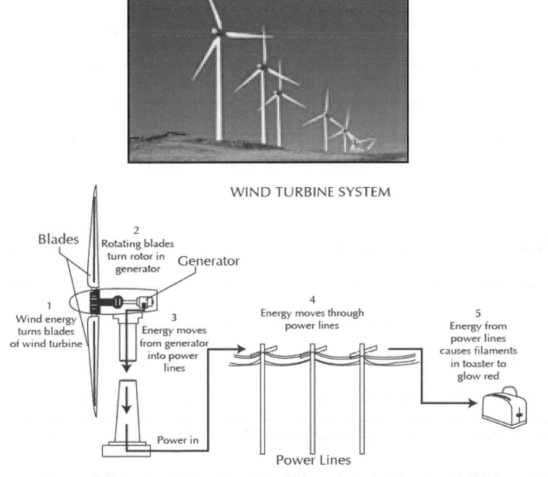

WIND TURBINE SYSTEM

Claim-Evidence-Reasoning

Prompt:

Write a scientific explanation for how the moving blades of the wind turbine help the toaster work.

Claim:

_____

_____

_____

Evidence:

_____

_____

_____

_____

_____

Reasoning:

_____

_____

_____

_____

_____

_____

Name: _____   Date: _____

California Instructional Segment
Mission Log

Mission Briefing

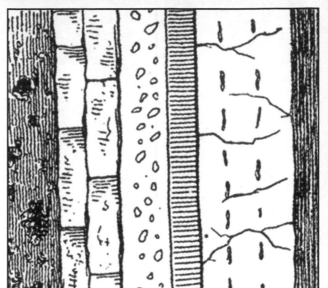

Anchoring Phenomena

How are landscapes sculpted over time?

Mission Briefing

You work for an animation company that is creating an app for students to simulate how landscapes could be sculpted by different events. Students would be able to pick the event and see how this section of rock changes.

- What factors affect how quickly landscapes change?

- How can people minimize the effects of changing landscape on property while still protecting the environment?

California Instructional Segment

Mission Log

Class Mission Log

Information Gained	Connection to Mission
Rock Patterns	**Rock Patterns**
How do rock layers and patterns tell a story?	What are some patterns you could see in layers of rock?
How are landscape changes recorded by layers of rocks and fossils?	What evidence is left behind in rock layers?
Changing Land	**Changing Land**
How can wind change the land over time?	What evidence of weathering, erosion, or deposition might be found in rock layers?
How can water change the land over time?	

California Instructional Segment

Mission Log

Class Mission Log

Information Gained	Connection to Mission
Changing Land, continued	**Changing Land, continued**
How can vegetation affect landscapes?	What evidence of vegetation could be found in layers of rock?
	_____
_____	_____
How do plant roots affect rocks?	_____
_____	**Plate Tectonics**
_____	What evidence could be left behind in the rock layers if an earthquake took place?
Plate Tectonics	_____
How can scientists predict where earthquakes might occur?	_____
_____	_____
_____	
What types of landforms can form when plates touch?	
_____	
_____	

California Instructional Segment
Mission Log

Class Mission Log

Information Gained

Natural Processes

What natural disasters occur in your area?

_____

_____

_____

Can the damage caused by natural disasters be minimized?

_____

_____

_____

_____

Connection to Mission

Natural Processes

When a volcano erupts, it can destroy the living things on the land. Once the lava cools, new rock layers are formed. On the picture below, draw what the volcano would look like after it erupted and new layers were formed.

Segment 3:
Sculpting
Landscapes

California Instructional Segment
Action Plan

Action Plan

Create illustrations for your animation company's new app to show how rock layers could change based on different events.

Here's what we know:

- Some changes that affect the appearance of sedimentary rock ayers are slow, while others are fast.

- When exposed to the elements, erosion can change the appearance of sedimentary rock.

- Sedimentary rock forms in layers, and the color and composition depend on the environment at that time.

California Instructional Segment

Action Plan

Take Action

How might the vegetation's roots affect the layers below the surface? Illustrate this change.

Original

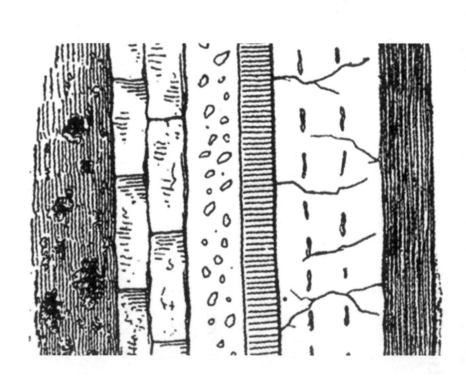

With Roots

California Instructional Segment

Action Plan

Take Action

If earthquakes shook the ground, how would they change the appearance of the layers? Illustrate this change.

Original

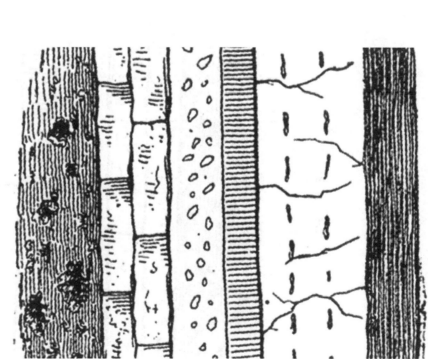

After Earthquakes

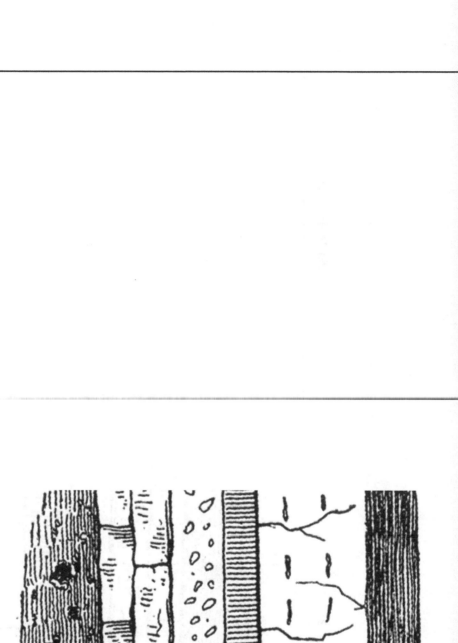

California Instructional Segment
Action Plan

Take Action

A nearby active volcano erupts and releases lava. How would this change the model? Illustrate showing this change.

Original

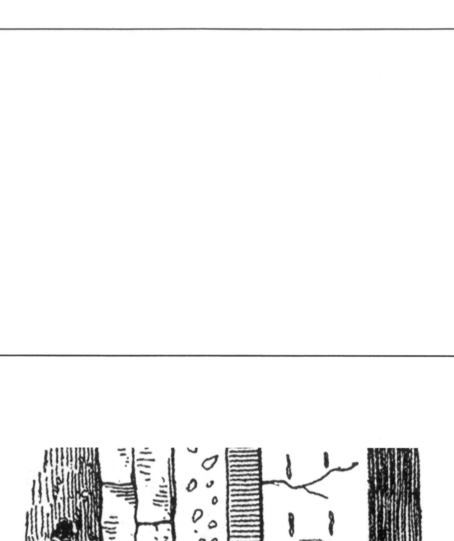

After Volcano

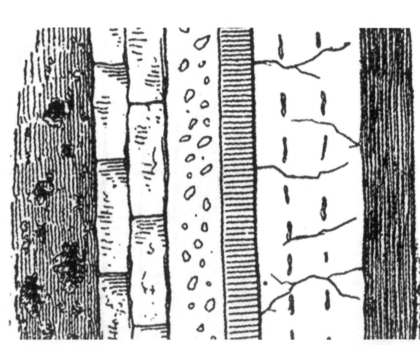

California Instructional Segment

Action Plan

Take Action

Part of the layers have been exposed to the surface and now can be changed by wind, water, waves, and ice. How would this change the appearance of the layers? Illustrate this change.

Original

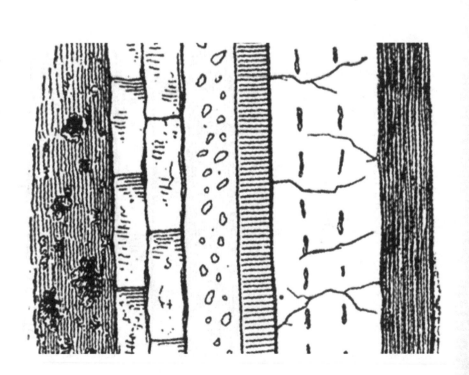

After Weathering, Erosion, and Deposition

California Instructional Segment

Action Plan

Take Action

What would the layers look like if someone chose all the events? How would the layers look after tree roots, an earthquake, a volcanic eruption, and exposure to weathering, erosion, and deposition? Illustrate this change.

Original

All the Events

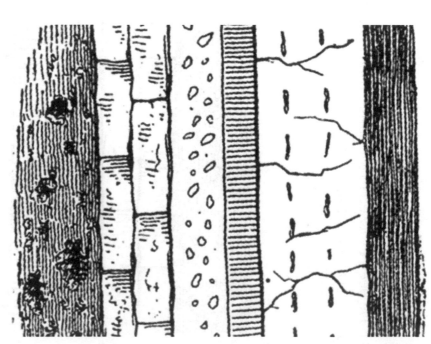

Rock Patterns

Name: _____ Date: _____

 # Graphic Organizer

Directions: Record information about rock layers and fossils below. Be sure to include information about how each indicates how the landscape has changed over time.

Rock Layers
Examples:

Fossils
Examples:

Name: _____   Date: _____

Explore 1

Rock Layers

Draw and label the layers and fossils.

Write a short description of each layer describing the type of fossil that was found in that layer and what the fossil says about the environment during that time.

Layer 1	Layer 2
_____	_____
_____	_____
_____	_____
Layer 3	**Layer 4**
_____	_____
_____	_____
_____	_____
_____	_____

Explore 1

Trade models with another group. Draw and label the layers and fossils.

Write a short description of each layer describing the type of fossil that was found in that layer and what the fossil says about the environment during that time.

Layer 1	Layer 2
Layer 3	**Layer 4**

Name: _____ Date: _____

 **Explore 1**

Rock Layers

Claim-Evidence-Reasoning

Using a scientific explanation, how can we use rock samples to describe what happened in Earth's past?

Claim:

_____

_____

_____

Evidence:

_____

_____

_____

_____

Reasoning:

_____

_____

_____

_____

_____

_____

_____

 **Explore 2**

Earthquake!

Draw the layers.

Before the earthquake	After the earthquake	With third layer added

1. How did the force of the earthquake affect the pattern of layers on your model?

_____

_____

_____

2. How would you know an earthquake had occurred if you observed the patterns in rock layers?

_____

_____

_____

3. How does this relate to the phenomena of how rocks can give us clues to the past?

_____

_____

_____

Explore 2

Earthquake!
Claim-Evidence-Reasoning

Using a scientific explanation, describe the relative age of rock layers.

Claim:

_____

_____

_____

Evidence:

_____

_____

_____

_____

Reasoning:

_____

_____

_____

_____

_____

_____

Name: _____   Date: _____

Linking Literacy
Pre-Reading

Preview and Predict

Before you read: Fill in the table below based on your preview of the text.

Preview	Predict
What is the title of this STEMscopedia?	What do you predict you will learn after reading the text?
Look at the pictures in the text. Draw one of your favorite pictures in the space below.	What topics will be included in the text?
Copy the first sentence on page 1, page 2, and page 3.	List two questions you will be able to answer after reading these pages.

Name: _____   Date: _____

Linking Literacy
During-Reading

Main Ideas and Details

While you read: Look for details that give more information about the three main ideas listed below. Write four details for every main idea.

Text Topic: **Rock Patterns**		
Page	Main Idea:	Detail 1
	Fossils are preserved parts or traces of animals or plants that lived in the past.	Detail 2
		Detail 3
		Detail 4

Linking Literacy

During-Reading

Page	Main Idea:	Detail 1	Detail 2
	The order of the fossils can tell the age of the fossils.	Detail 3	Detail 4

Page	Main Idea:	Detail 1	Detail 2
	We can determine the actual age of fossils.	Detail 3	Detail 4

Rock Patterns

Linking Literacy
Post-Reading

Fossil Story Comic Strip

Directions: Draw a formation of fossil layers. On the lines below, describe what is happening and show which layer is the oldest and which is the youngest. Label your drawing and identify the fossil.

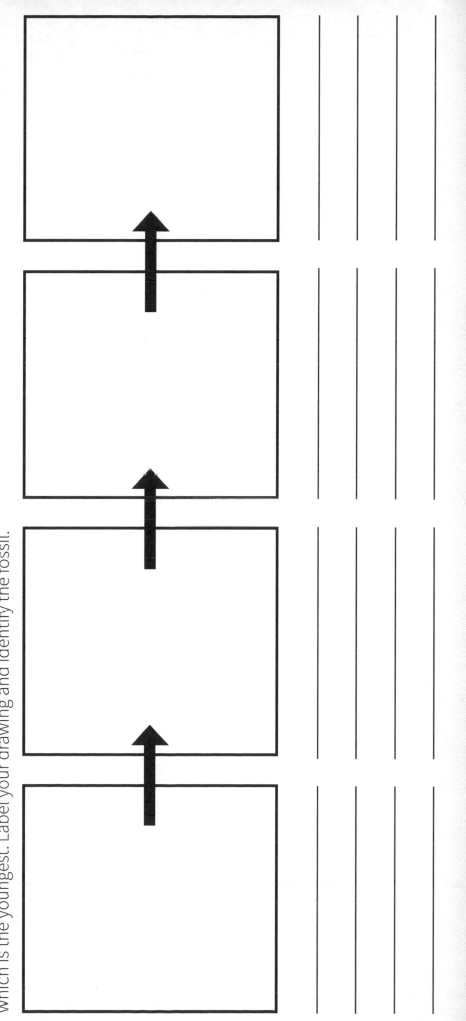

Reading Science

The Changing Surface of Earth

1. We may not notice it during our lifetime, but Earth's surface is always changing. The movements of ice, water, and wind cause these changes. These movements break down landforms, carry away the pieces, and deposit them in new places, creating new landforms in the process.

2. In many places on Earth, you can find masses of ice called *glaciers*. These glaciers are so huge, they look as if they are standing still, but they are actually floating slowly through valleys between mountains. As it moves, a glacier can erode the edges of a valley, making it wider and deeper. Glacial valleys have a rounded *U* shape.

3. In addition to eroding the edges of a valley, the great weight of a glacier can crush surface rocks beneath it. The pieces of broken rock are called *glacial sediments*. They can range in size from boulders to fine clay. As a glacier moves, it carries these sediments with it. When the glacier stops moving, the sediments are dumped, creating land formations. One of these landforms is known as a *moraine*, a hilly structure that can form at the edge of a glacier.

4. Water can also change Earth's surface. Rushing rivers cut through the land around them to form canyons. Canyons are narrow valleys created by erosion.

5. Besides **carving** the land, moving water can create new land features. As a river nears the sea, the land becomes more level. The river's energy is reduced, and its flow becomes sluggish. Like glaciers, rivers also carry pieces of rock and sand, called *sediments*. As the river slows near the sea, it deposits its load of sediments to create a delta. Deltas are broad, fan-shaped areas that are formed where rivers empty into standing water.

Reading Science

6. Moving air has less mass than ice or water; however, it can still shape Earth's surface. Winds can pick up small pieces of dirt or sand, often bouncing them along through the air. When these **particles** meet an obstacle, they pile up to form a dune. A dune is a hill of sand built by the wind. Coastal dunes form parallel to a shoreline and inland from a beach. They can help protect low-lying, inland areas from violent storm waves. However, the wind that builds a dune can also move it. Some desert dunes can travel more than 100 meters in a year.

7. From valleys and canyons to deltas and dunes, the forces of ice, water, and wind are constantly changing Earth's surface.

# Reading Science

1. The main idea of this passage is–

    A. ice can break down and build up Earth's landscape.

    B. water can change Earth's surface.

    C. wind can shape Earth's landforms.

    D. Earth's surface is always changing.

2. Which natural forces can create sediments?

    A. Wind and ice

    B. Moving air and moving water

    C. Water and ice

    D. Sunlight

3. According to paragraph 6, **particles** can pile up to form a dune. The word **_particles_** means–

    A. a hill of sand.

    B. large masses of ice.

    C. small pieces of matter.

    D. low-lying areas.

4. What can the reader infer from the passage?

    A.   Changes in Earth's surface occur slowly.

    B.   Glaciers are dangerous.

    C.   A person can see glaciers move.

    D.   Dunes last forever once they are formed.

5. What does the author mean by the word *carving* in paragraph 5 of the passage?

    A.   Creating sediments

    B.   Making new mountains

    C.   Cutting through land

    D.   Dropping sediments

Name: _____ Date: _____

∞ Open-Ended Response

1. You are an archeologist who just found a fossil of a nautilus shell. As you keep digging, you discover a prehistoric fish. What can you conclude about the age of the nautilus shell in relation to the fish fossil?

_____

_____

_____

_____

2. The Andes Mountains in South America contain dozens of fossils of marine animals. How might you have described the landscape of the Andes mountain area long ago?

_____

_____

_____

3. Imagine you are an archeologist who has just uncovered the fossil of an unidentified creature with large teeth and sharp claws. Describe this creature and give information about its habitat and diet. Be creative!

_____

_____

_____

_____

Claim-Evidence-Reasoning

Scenario:

A new interstate highway is being built near a fault line! Construction workers, while making room for the new road, cut through the side of a hill. The drawing below shows what they observed.

External Data:

Prompt:

Write a scientific explanation describing the characteristics of the environment and any events that took place while layer C was forming.

Claim:

_____

_____

_____

_____

Claim-Evidence-Reasoning

Evidence:

_____

_____

_____

_____

_____

_____

_____

_____

Reasoning:

_____

_____

_____

_____

_____

_____

_____

_____

_____

Changing Land

Name: _____ Date: _____

Graphic Organizer

Directions

List the agents of weathering and erosion inside the arrow as the **cause**. List the **effects** of the agents in the boxes.

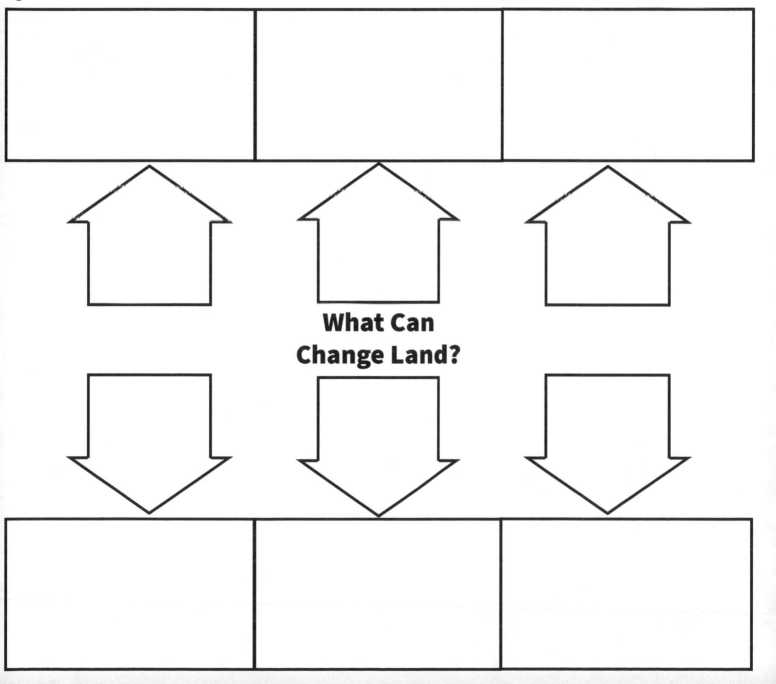

What Can Change Land?

Name: _____ Date: _____

🪝 Hook

Shake It

1. Fill the first jar halfway with water.

2. Fill the second jar halfway with pebbles (aquarium rocks).

3. Place a sugar cube in each container.

4. Secure the lids back on both jars.

5. Put on safety goggles.

6. Shake each container for one minute.

7. Allow jars to settle and observe.

8. Record your observation below.

Sugar cubes with water	**Sugar cubes with aquarium rocks**

 **Hook**

1. What do you notice about the sugar cubes in each jar?

2. What do you notice at the bottom of each jar?

3. Did the rocks or the water break down the sugar cube the most?

4. Which jar produced sediments?

Explore 1

Waves on the Beach

Our Driving Question:

How do waves affect a beach?

What We Need:

1 Computer and projector to view video (per class)
1 Watertight, shoe box-sized container
3 Small houses, blocks, toys, or objects
1 Craft stick

4 Cups of sand
Water
1 Ruler

Procedure:

1. Fill the shoe box-sized container with about one inch of water. Let it stand until it is still.

2. Add sand to one end of the container until it rises above the water level.

3. Place toys or objects along the shore of your beach.

4. Pick one location on the beach where all measurements will be taken throughout the activity.

5. Measure the height of the sand and make a scientific drawing of the beach. Record your observations in the first box of the data table on the next page.

6. Move the craft stick in the water back and forth for 10 seconds, making small waves.

7. Measure how high the sand is and make a scientific drawing of the beach. Record your observations in the second box of the data table on the next page.

8. Move the craft stick in the water back and forth with more force for 30 seconds, creating bigger waves.

Explore 1

9. Measure how high the sand is and make a scientific drawing of the beach. Record your observations in the third box of the data table on page two of your Student Journal.

Sand measurement before making waves	Make a scientific drawing of the beach before making waves.
Sand measurement after 10 seconds of making waves	Make a scientific drawing of the beach after 10 seconds of making waves.
Sand measurement after 30 seconds of making waves	Make a scientific drawing of the beach after 30 seconds of making waves.

Reflections and Conclusions:

How did the waves change the beach?

_____

_____

_____

As a result of your investigation, what is one cause of beach erosion and its effect on beaches?

_____

_____

_____

Explore 1

Waves on the Beach
Claim-Evidence-Reasoning

Using scientific reasoning, explain how wave action affects the size of the beach.

Claim:

_____

_____

Evidence:

_____

_____

_____

_____

Reasoning:

_____

_____

_____

_____

_____

Explore 2

What Processes Can Change Land?

Part I: Wind

Paper Color	Lightly Fan for 5 Seconds	Lightly Fan for 10 Seconds	Quickly Fan for 5 Seconds	Quickly Fan for 10 Seconds

Use the data in the table to answer the following questions.

1. Explain how the speed of the wind and how long it blew affected the movement of the paper.

_____

_____

2. Where do you see examples of erosion and deposition? Explain your answer.

_____

_____

3. Predict what would happen if you fanned quickly for 15 seconds. Explain your reasoning.

_____

_____

_____

Explore 2

Part II: Ice

Record all data in the table below.

	Before	**Small Ice Chip**	**Medium Ice Cube**	**Large Ice Block**
Drawing				
Width of the Groove (cm)				

Use the data to answer the questions below.

1. What did the ice do to your mountain?

_____

_____

2. Explain where you saw erosion and deposition being modeled in this activity.

_____

_____

3. How did the size of the ice affect the amount of sand that was eroded?

_____

_____

4. What would happen if you pushed an even larger block of ice down the mountain? Explain your reasoning.

_____

_____

_____

Explore 2

Part III: Vegetation

	Before	After
Pushing the toothpick into the top of the cookie		
Pushing the toothpick through the bottom of the cookie		

Use the data to answer the questions below.

1. What did the toothpick do to the cookie?

_____

_____

2. Explain where you observed weathering and erosion in this model.

_____

_____

3. What was left on the paper plate? What process does this represent?

_____

_____

4. What would happen if multiple toothpicks were pushed into the cookie at the same time?

_____

_____

_____

Explore 2

Part IV: Application

Reference the pictures to answer the questions in the table below.

Picture 1	Picture 2
What is happening in the picture?	**What is happening in the picture?**
How is it similar to a model you have seen in class?	How is it similar to a model you have seen in class?
How is it different from a model you have seen in class?	How is it different from a model you have seen in class?

Explore 2

Picture 3

What is happening in the picture?

_____

_____

How is it similar to a model you have seen in class?

_____

_____

How is it different from a model you have seen in class?

_____

_____

Picture 4

What is happening in the picture?

_____

_____

How is it similar to a model you have seen in class?

_____

_____

How is it different from a model you have seen in class?

_____

_____

Picture 5

What is happening in the picture?

_____

_____

How is it similar to a model you have seen in class?

_____

_____

How is it different from a model you have seen in class?

_____

_____

Picture 6

What is happening in the picture?

_____

_____

How is it similar to a model you have seen in class?

_____

_____

How is it different from a model you have seen in class?

_____

_____

🔍 Explore 3

Rushing Water

Our Driving Question:

How does the type of soil and slope of an area affect the rate of erosion?

What We Need:

3 Textbooks

2 Aluminum 11" x 13" cake pans

1 Large tub

1 Squeeze-top bottle

1 ½ Cups of water

6 Cups of soil

½ Cup of rye grass seed

Procedure:

1. Pour 3 cups of soil into the other aluminum cake pan.

2. Place one textbook on the table. Place the edge of the aluminum cake pan with just soil on the edge of the book so that one end of the cake pan is elevated and so that the pan slopes to the table.

3. Pour ½ cup of water into the squeeze-top bottle.

4. Hold the squeeze-top bottle over the middle of the elevated end of the cake pan. Slowly squeeze the water onto the soil in the cake pan. Observe what happens. How fast did the water flow?

5. Record on the data table on the next page.

6. Stack two books on the table. Elevate the end of the cake pan.

Explore 3

7. Pour ½ cup of water into the squeeze-top bottle.

8. Hold the squeeze-top bottle over the middle of the elevated end of the cake pan. Slowly squeeze the water onto the soil in the cake pan. Observe what happens.

9. Record on the data table on the next page.

10. Stack three books on the table. Elevate the end of the cake pan.

11. Pour ½ cup of water into the squeeze-top bottle.

12. Hold the squeeze-top bottle over the middle of the elevated end of the aluminum cake pan. Slowly squeeze the water onto the soil in the cake pan. Observe what happens.

13. Record on the data table below.

14. Repeat the same tests on the pan with the grass and record your observations on the data table on the next page.

15. Answer the reflection questions at the end of this Student Journal.

Record your data and observations while testing the pan with **soil only**.

Amount of Water	Height of Slope	Rate of Flow	Observation

Explore 3

Record your data and observations while testing the pan with **grassy soil**.

Amount of Water	Height of Slope	Rate of Flow	Observation

 **Explore 3**

Reflection Questions:

1. What happened to the soil when the water was added?

_____

_____

_____

2. What did the moving water form in the pan with soil only?

_____

_____

_____

3. What is the relationship between the slope of the pan and the rate of flow of the water?

_____

_____

_____

4. How does this compare to rainfall falling on the land?

_____

_____

_____

5. How did the grass affect the rate of erosion? Explain.

_____

_____

_____

Explore 3

Rushing Water
Claim-Evidence-Reasoning

Prompt 1:

Using scientific reasoning, explain how the slope of the land affects the erosion from rainfall.

Claim:

_____

_____

_____

Evidence:

_____

_____

_____

_____

Reasoning:

_____

_____

_____

_____

_____

 **Explore 3**

Rushing Water
Claim-Evidence-Reasoning

Prompt 2:

Using scientific reasoning, explain the effect the grassy soil had on erosion from water.

Claim:

_____

_____

_____

Evidence:

_____

_____

_____

_____

Reasoning:

_____

_____

_____

_____

_____

_____

Name: _____ Date: _____

Linking Literacy
Pre-Reading

Changing Land Comic Strip

Directions: Draw a four-panel comic strip that shows the land being changed by wind, water, or ice. Describe your comic below.

What caused the changes to the land in your comic? _____

How did the land change over time? _____

_____

_____

Linking Literacy
During-Reading

Compare and Contrast

As you read, pay close attention to changes to land that are caused by forces of nature vs. changes caused by plants and animals. Record examples and a short description or example of these changes in the circles below.

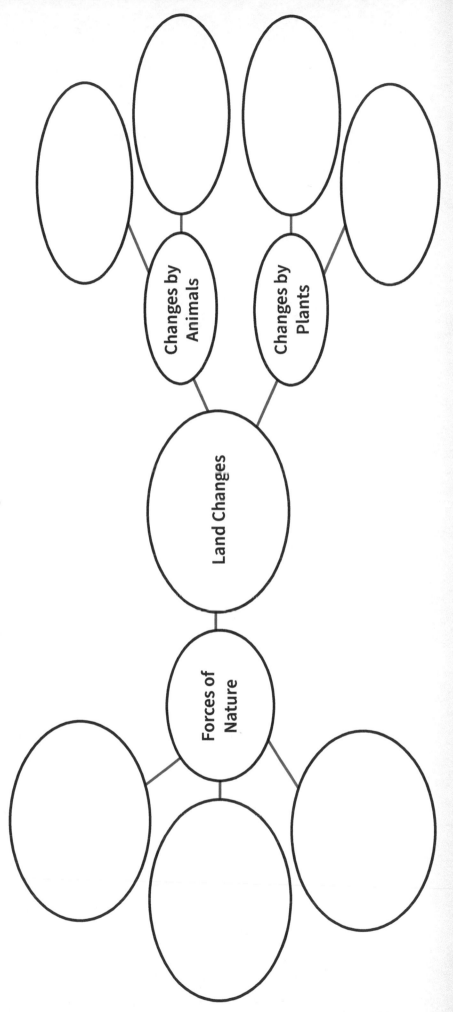

Name: _____ Date: _____

Linking Literacy
Post-Reading

Four-Corner Summary

Directions: Copy the following onto a note card. Using the text or notes from the text, write four facts about land changes. Then turn each fact into a sentence, forming a paragraph on the back of the note card.

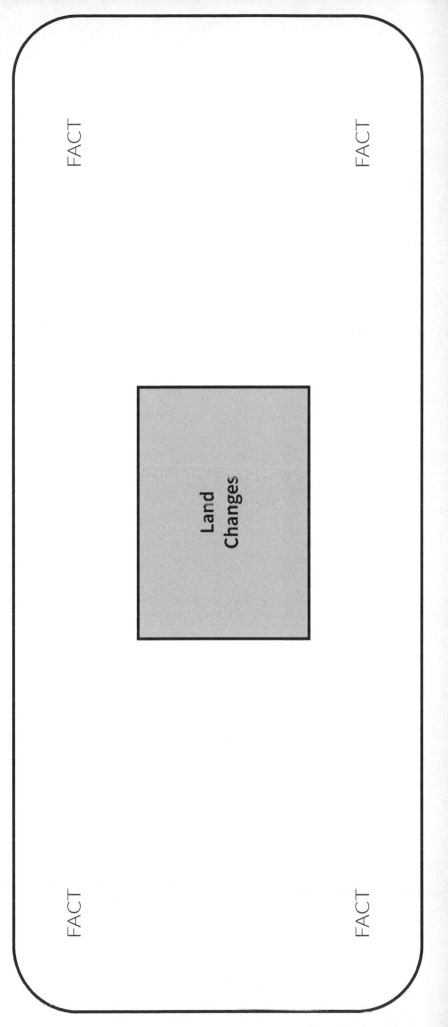

FACT

FACT

Land Changes

FACT

FACT

Reading Science

Water: One of Earth's Most Powerful Forces

1. Placed in the middle of Eastern Iowa was Lake Delhi. Lake Delhi was a man-made lake built in 1922. It was built on the Maquoketa River. The lake was enjoyed by many. People went boating and fishing on the lake. Over the years, many people built cabins along the lake. It had become a home and a playground for many.

2. Lake Delhi was built using an embankment dam. An embankment dam is made of clay, rock, sand, and soil. The Lake Delhi dam also had a concrete part where spillway gates sat. It also had electricity-producing turbines.

3. The lake's dam was originally used to produce hydroelectricity. Hydroelectricity is created from the flow of water. The dam stopped working in 1968 and was never fixed. It had not produced electricity since then. Other parts of the dam were taken care of. Parts were replaced and floodgates were checked. The dam was going through repairs to cracks in early 2010.

4. The summer of 2010 was very rainy in Eastern Iowa. In July, a period of heavy rain hit Eastern Iowa. The area saw 10 inches of rain in 12 hours. Dam operators opened two of the three floodgates. Floodgates are opened to release water buildup. Opening the gates lets water flow out slowly to reduce flooding. The third floodgate was not working correctly. It was partly opened.

5. As more water built up, the dam was in danger; it could not hold back the huge amount of water. Water ran over the top of the dam. It caused a 200-foot section of the dam to erode. The force of the water also destroyed the road that crossed the dam. The concrete road was broken up into smaller pieces and flowed downstream. The water flowed out of the lake and took soil with it. It changed the landscape that surrounded the lake. Trees were carried downstream.

6. Citizens downstream heard the news. They were evacuated. They left their homes. They feared that the great amount of water would take their lives. Watchers downstream saw boats, homes, hay bales, and even cows floating down the mighty Maquoketa.

7. Thankfully, not many people lived around the area that flowed downstream of Lake Delhi. The area was largely farm ground. As the water flowed out of the lake, water soaked into farm fields. This caused crops to be destroyed. Farms and homes were flooded. After the water **receded**, farmers found dead fish and parts of homes and boats in their fields.

8. The lake has been drained since that day. All that is left now is the Maquoketa River. There is now a large hole where the lake once was. Citizens have made a committee. They want to rebuild the dam. They also want to restore the dam's ability to make hydroelectricity.

9. The story of Lake Delhi is one that shows Earth's greatest force at work. The impact of the draining lake and eroded dam is still told by residents in the area. It is a story they won't soon forget.

Reading Science

1. How does the author organize this piece of text to help the reader understand it better?

    A.   By describing the effects of water weathering

    B.   By telling the cause and effects of water weathering

    C.   By sequencing the events of water weathering

    D.   By discussing the problem of the Lake Delhi dam and how the residents responded to it

2. What does the word **receded** mean?

    A.   To draw back or withdraw from a point

    B.   To slope backward

    C.   To become greater

    D.   To prolong

Reading Science

3. What environmental factor caused the dam to break?

    A. The concrete that was used to build it

    B. The third floodgate that was not working properly

    C. The dam that was made out of clay, sand, soil, and rock

    D. The eroded soil that flowed over the dam

4. What can the reader infer about building dams in 1922 versus building dams today?

    A. They are built the same way.

    B. They are built with the same materials today.

    C. They are not checked for malfunctions today.

    D. They are built with stronger materials today.

Reading Science

5. The author wrote this passage–

    A.   to inform the reader about how water changes the land.

    B.   to describe what happened when a dam broke.

    C.   to sequence the events of the breaching of a dam.

    D.   to persuade people to build stronger dams today.

6. Which sentence supports the statement, "Water and gravity break rocks, soil, and sediment and move them around"?

    A.   *The dam was in danger; it could not hold back the huge amount of water.*

    B.   *When the water receded, farmers found dead fish and parts of homes and boats in their fields.*

    C.   *The water flowed out of the lake and took soil with it.*

    D.   *The concrete road was broken up into smaller pieces and flowed downstream.*

Reading Science

7. Which important piece of information would the reader want others to know from reading this passage?

    A.   Water can harm plants and animals.

    B.   Humans can have an impact on their environment.

    C.   Water's powerful force can cause erosion and flooding that changes Earth's landscape.

    D.   Dams should be built out of strong materials so they do not breach.

∞ Open-Ended Response

1. After a heavy rain, you notice soil from your flower beds has washed into the street. Explain what happened and why it happened.

_____

_____

_____

_____

2. What environment do you think will become eroded faster—a beach with tall grasses and shrubs or a beach with many sand dunes and no grass? Explain your thinking.

_____

_____

_____

_____

3. Deserts experience a lot of wind erosion. Describe the relationship between rainfall, vegetation (plants), and erosion in the desert.

_____

_____

_____

_____

Claim-Evidence-Reasoning

Changing Land

Scenario:

The photographs below show the same location, but were taken at different times. Compare the two images.

External Data:

| Initial photograph | Later photograph |

Prompt:

Write a scientific explanation for the changes that happened to the rocks over the years.

Claim:

_____

_____

_____

_____

_____

Claim-Evidence-Reasoning

Evidence:

_____
_____
_____
_____
_____
_____
_____
_____

Reasoning:

_____
_____
_____
_____
_____
_____
_____
_____
_____
_____
_____
_____

Plate Tectonics

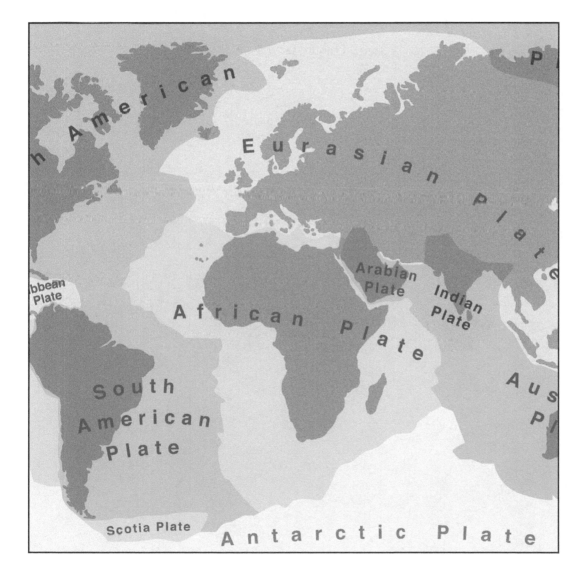

Name: _____ Date: _____

Graphic Organizer

Where in the World?

Directions

Draw and label at least one location where there is a mountain range, a volcano, and a high chance of earthquakes. Write a brief description about why it is located in that spot.

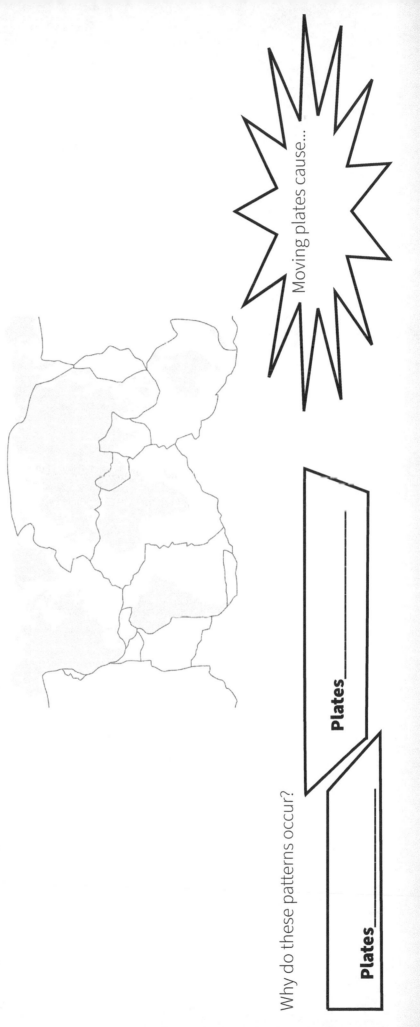

Moving plates cause...

Why do these patterns occur?

Plates _____

Plates _____

Explore 1

Patterns in Land

Make observations from the maps and record them using the world map outline. Use your observations to answer the questions below.

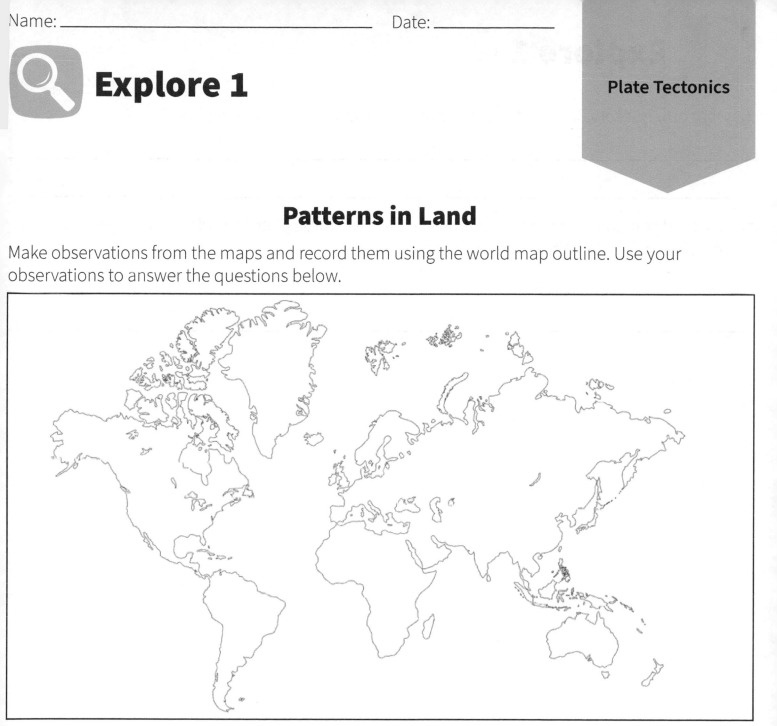

1. What landforms do you see? What events did you notice?

_____

_____

2. Looking at the map, what can you conclude was the reason for the earthquake that occurred near Japan?

_____

_____

Explore 1

3. What other observations did you make about the continents and the plates?

_____

_____

4. What did you notice about the relationship between these plate boundaries and the landforms you observed? What about the earthquakes?

_____

_____

Explore 1

Patterns in Land

Claim-Evidence-Reasoning

Use the information you gathered during the activity to answer this question:

What is the relationship between tectonic plate boundaries and landforms and events? State your claim and provide specific evidence and reasoning for your answer.

Claim:

_____

_____

_____

Evidence:

_____

_____

_____

_____

Reasoning:

_____

_____

_____

_____

Name: _____ Date: _____

Explore 2

Tectonic Plates

Use the space below to draw and label your tectonic plate model.

Movement	Observations	Event Being Modeled
Plates slide past each other.		
Plates move toward each other.		
Plates move away from each other.		

How could maps help you identify where tectonic plate boundaries are?

_____

_____

_____

Describe the relationship between certain landforms and the motion of tectonic plates.

_____

_____

_____

Linking Literacy
During-Reading

Claim and Evidence

Evidence	Evidence

Claim

Plate movement causes a change in land.

Evidence	Evidence

Linking Literacy
Post-Reading

3-2-1 Summary

Directions: Fill in the table below after reading the text.

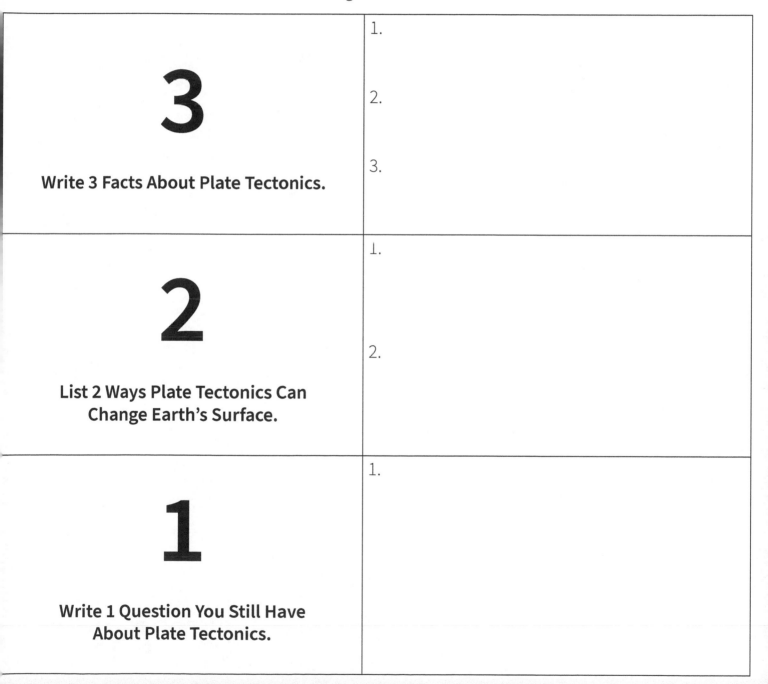

3 **Write 3 Facts About Plate Tectonics.**	1. 2. 3.
2 **List 2 Ways Plate Tectonics Can Change Earth's Surface.**	1. 2.
1 **Write 1 Question You Still Have About Plate Tectonics.**	1.

📖 **Reading Science**

The Hiking Trip

1. Pablo and Rafael were setting out on a hiking trip with their Uncle George. They were planning to climb a small mountain. It was the first time for both boys. They could not wait.

2. They had packed in their backpacks everything they needed for their day of hiking. Inside their backpacks were sandwiches, water, sunglasses, sunscreen, and long-sleeve T-shirts.

3. Before they started on their journey, they gathered around a tree with their uncle. Uncle George showed them the inside of his backpack. He had a first aid kit, a headlamp, extra water bottles, and a bunch of folded-up papers.

4. "What are all those papers for?" asked Pablo.

5. "Oh, these?" replied Uncle George. He pulled the papers out of his pack. "These are maps. They are going to show us the trail we will use and where we are headed."

6. "Why do we need a map? Can't we just use the phone?" asked Rafael.

7. "Well, we can do that, too," replied Uncle George. "But, just in case our phone battery loses power, we will have the maps as a backup. These maps will also show us trails for this park that the phone might not show us." Uncle George unfolded the map and pointed to an exact spot. "We are right here, and this is where we are headed," he said. Uncle George pointed to the mountain range to the right of them. It was on the map in the exact location.

8. The boys adjusted their backpacks, put on their sunglasses, and tied their shoes tight. They set off, following Uncle George on the trail.

9. They passed trees and birds as they hiked up the mountainside. After about an hour, they came to a river. As they crossed over the river, Rafael asked, "Uncle George, you know how you can see where Earth's features are on the map? Are there maps of the bottom of the ocean?"

10. "Yes, bigger bodies of water are often mapped out," explained Uncle George. "If you are exploring in the ocean and want to find an underwater volcano, maps often show where those are located under the water. Maps can also show an open **crevice**. Some crevices in the ocean can be up to 10 feet wide."

11. "In school, we learned that Earth's surface is always changing. Our teacher said Earth is made up of plates," said Pablo. The boys got out their water bottles as they stopped to rest under a tree.

12. "Plates?" asked Rafael. "You mean plates like we eat on?"

13. Uncle George laughed. "No, not those kinds of plates. When we think of Earth's plates, we think more like big puzzle pieces. These plates move very slowly. They can cause changes to Earth. Scientists created maps many years ago. If we were to compare those maps with today's maps, we would see countries and islands in slightly different places. Landmasses broke apart."

14. "So, maps change, then?" asked Rafael.

15. "Yes, maps have to be updated to show change. For example, the mountain we are about to climb is part of the Rocky Mountain range. It was not here millions of years ago. It formed due to tectonic plates pushing up against each other and pushing Earth's land and crust up. These mountains are no longer growing, but they were many, many years ago," explained Uncle George. "Volcanoes are formed in the same way and are sometimes part of mountain ranges. Most mountain ranges form along the edges of continents, where the land meets the ocean, but some also form inland. These changes do not occur fast, however. They are very slow changes."

16. "Earthquakes happen very fast," said Pablo.

17. "They sure do," replied Uncle George. "Earthquakes happen quickly. The plates move in different directions. Scientists can measure the movement of plates and can sometimes predict when an earthquake is coming, as they sometimes come in patterns."

18. "That's scary," both boys responded.

19. "It is, but it just shows you how powerful Earth's movements are," replied Uncle George. "Without the moving of the plates, we wouldn't have this mountain to climb."

20. The boys looked up the mountain in amazement after hearing Uncle George's lesson on Earth's changing surface. As they finished their water and grabbed a quick snack, they were ready to continue their climb. Uncle George got out his camera and took a picture of the boys so they could show their mom their accomplishment. They would always remember their special day hiking with Uncle George and learning about the amazing Earth.

Reading Science

1. The movement of Earth's plates has changed the way that Earth looks over many years. What evidence supports this?

   A. "Earthquakes happen very fast."

   B. *"Maps have to be updated to show change."*

   C. Maps of many years ago show countries and islands in different places.

   D. Volcanoes can be a part of mountain ranges.

2. Based on the information Uncle George explains, what can be concluded about the impact of the movement of Earth's plates?

   A. The movement of Earth's plates does not affect where land and oceans are placed.

   B. The movement of Earth's plates affects the location of oceans only.

   C. The movement of Earth's plates affects the location of islands only.

   D. The movement of Earth's plates affects the location of land and oceans.

3. Uncle George compares Earth to puzzle pieces. Why does he do this?

   A. To show that Earth's plates are complicated

   B. To show that Earth's plates fit together like a puzzle

   C. To show that Earth's plates can be put together by humans

   D. To show that Earth's plates create beautiful pictures

Reading Science

4. What is a synonym for the word **crevice**?

    A.   Wide

    B.   Trench

    C.   Closure

    D.   Juncture

5. The reader can conclude that tectonic plates–

    A.   are the reason Earth has mountain ranges.

    B.   are located in the middle of continents.

    C.   are the cause of rivers on mountains.

    D.   move very quickly.

∞ Open-Ended Response

1. Describe the most likely relationship between these mountains and nearby tectonic plates.

_____

_____

_____

_____

2. Is there a pattern to the locations of earthquakes and volcanoes around the globe? Explain.

_____

_____

_____

_____

3. What landforms would you most likely see at the edges of plate boundaries in the ocean?

_____

_____

_____

_____

Claim-Evidence-Reasoning

Plate Tectonics

Scenario:

A large number of earthquakes and volcanic eruptions occur in the basin of the Pacific Ocean. This area is known as the Ring of Fire. The Ring of Fire has 452 volcanoes and is home to over 90% of the world's active and dormant volcanoes.

External Data:

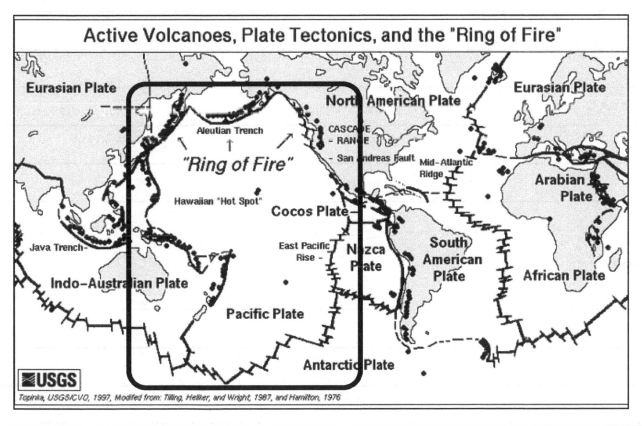

Prompt:

Using scientific explanation and the information provided on the map, explain why the Ring of Fire developed where it did.

Claim-Evidence-Reasoning

Claim:

_____

_____

_____

_____

Evidence:

_____

_____

_____

_____

_____

_____

Reasoning:

_____

_____

_____

_____

_____

_____

_____

Natural Processes

Graphic Organizer

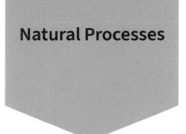

Saving the City!

Directions

For each natural process, define the process, then list steps humans can take to reduce their impact.

Natural Process	Definition	Ways to Reduce Impact
Tsunami		
Flood		
Earthquake		
Volcanic Eruption		

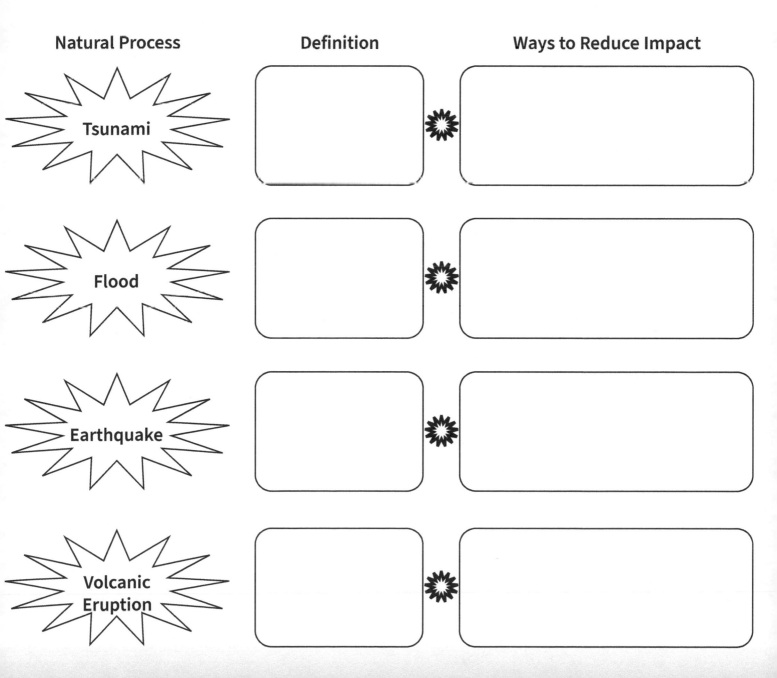

Explore 1

Safety First!

Write the three most important sentences from the information about each natural hazard. Be sure to include sentences that tell what each natural hazard is and what impact it has.

Tsunami	Earthquake
Flood	Volcano

Explore 1

Put an X in the box by the safety suggestions that would help reduce the impact of each natural hazard.

Safety Suggestions	Earthquake	Flood	Tsunami	Volcanic Eruption
Either block or allow massive amounts of water through structures.				
Watch news and weather reports.				
Reinforce buildings with concrete.				
Put buildings on stilts.				
Have an early-warning system.				
Build flexible structures.				
Don't build in areas where natural hazards are likely.				
Have an emergency plan in place.				
Have an emergency kit with food, supplies, and first aid materials.				

Explore 1

Quickly sketch what you would like the safety poster to look like. Discuss your ideas together as a group. Be sure to include the name of the natural hazard and ways people can help reduce its impact. Your poster can include words, pictures, or a combination of both.

Explore 1

Safety First

Claim-Evidence-Reasoning

Use the information you gathered during the activity to complete the following task.

Write a scientific explanation describing why we should be prepared for floods, earthquakes, tsunamis, and volcanic eruptions. State your claim and provide specific evidence and reasoning for your answer.

Claim:

_____

_____

_____

Evidence:

_____

_____

_____

Reasoning:

_____

_____

_____

_____

_____

_____

🔍 Explore 2

Volcano Island

The Problem

You have just won an island! Unfortunately, there are some dangers associated with owning an island. It is located on top of a volcano, which could cause earthquakes. You are surrounded by ocean, so large waves from tsunamis and floods from major storms are possible. You need a place to live that will keep you and your family safe.

The Challenge

Design a structure that will keep you and your family safe from any possible volcanos, earthquakes, tsunamis, and floods.

Criteria and Constraints

- You can research the best possible structure for different natural processes to help you design a safe place to live.

- You must draw and label a design for your structure before beginning to build it.

- The structure should have as little impact as possible on the natural environment.

- The structure must be able to withstand small earthquakes.

- The structure must be able to withstand volcanos.

- The structure must be able to withstand large waves and flooding from tsunamis.

- The structure must be able to keep humans alive as they wait for the disaster to end.

- You must decide what the actual dimensions of the structure should be to hold a family of four.

Explore 2

Brainstorm and Research

Write down any ideas you have about how you could master the challenge. If you need more information, write down what you need to know and gain permission from your teacher to research the answer.

Design Plan

Use the ideas you wrote down while brainstorming to develop a final design plan. Draw your plan and label the parts. Be sure to list what each part is made of.

Explore 2

Build and Test

Build your design and test it. Does it meet all the criteria and constraints? Use the space below to list what problems you need to fix in your design.

_____

_____

_____

_____

Refine and Redesign

How could you solve the problems you found during testing? Use the space below to draw your new design that should solve the problems.

Retest and Finalize

Build and test your new design. Does it meet all the criteria and constraints? If not, repeat the refine and redesign process. If it does, move on to planning your presentation.

Presentation Plan

Use the space below to plan how you will present your final product. Be sure to include who will speak and what you want to say. Your presentation should include the scientific ideas used to solve this design challenge.

Name: _____ Date: _____

Linking Literacy
During-Reading

Emergency Preparedness

Directions: While reading, find the natural process in the text and fill in the effect. Then describe a way that humans can prepare for each natural process.

Natural Process	Effect on Human Life	How We Can Prepare
Tsunami →		
Volcanic eruption →		
Earthquake →		
Flood →		

Linking Literacy
Post-Reading

Plan of Action

Directions: Choose one natural disaster that could occur in your area. Create a plan of action for your family. Be sure to include the following:

- Why the disaster is dangerous
- What you will do to prepare for the disaster
- What you will do if the disaster happens

Disaster	
Why is it dangerous?	
How will you prepare?	
What will you do if it happens?	

📖 Reading Science

Amazing Earth

1. Our planet is amazing. A tiny seed grows into a tree. Water runs in rivers. A storm forms and then a rainbow shines. Sometimes, though, nature can be disastrous. Sometimes Earth cracks, slips, and slides. The hot matter inside oozes out. Strong waves of water cause damage. These disasters change Earth and the living things on it. Volcanoes erupt, and earthquakes shake. Tsunamis and avalanches occur. Sometimes, one disaster can cause another.

Volcanoes

2. A crack forms in Earth and creates a vent. The vent lets out hot magma and ash. Volcanoes form where Earth's plates come together or move apart. A volcano happens when Earth's crust ruptures, or breaks apart, allowing the magma and ash to escape. This is often a violent eruption with magma and ash spewing high into the air.

3. Volcanoes cannot be stopped. Humans can, however, lower the effects of volcanoes by not building near them. It's important to have a volcanologist, someone who studies volcanoes, to help communities know and predict the behavior of volcanoes. The volcanologists let citizens know when the volcano may explode. Humans can try to build rock walls to stop lava. People can also know when to vacate to prevent death.

Earthquakes

4. Sometimes, Earth's plates slip and slide. This causes an earthquake. Imagine pulling a tablecloth off a table that is set for dinner. The cloth comes off. Glasses of water spill, plates slide off, and silverware shakes. This is similar to the motion an earthquake causes. Earth's plates slide past each other. This makes the ground shake. These shifts in Earth are studied by seismologists.

5. Earthquakes cannot be stopped. It is important to know if earthquakes occur where you live. Southern California is on a crack in Earth. People prepare for earthquakes. They make sure to build strong buildings. They check for dangers in their homes. They have supplies ready. Family members know about safe zones. They also have emergency plans.

Tsunamis

6. A volcano erupts under the ocean. It makes the water move. It creates a huge wave. The same happens with an earthquake underwater. A huge wave moves through the water. It moves until it stops on land. This is a tsunami. The wave moves until it reaches land, where it damages many objects.

7. Tsunamis are a part of nature. People who live near the coast feel tsunamis. Some communities build dikes that help absorb the giant waves. Scientists are learning more about tsunamis so they can hopefully build a warning system. It would warn people to move inland. Building communities away from the coast would also help lower the effect of tsunamis.

Avalanches

8. An avalanche starts when snow on a mountain builds up. Some think that a noise can start an avalanche. That is a **myth**. An avalanche is very unsafe, because if caught in one, it can bury you. Sometimes, people are rescued.

9. People must stay away from areas where avalanches may occur. Park rangers will let hikers or skiers know if there is an avalanche risk. Park rangers check the snow and start avalanches on purpose when no one is close. People should move together in the mountains and take with them a small shovel and a light. They should have a stick to check how safe it is to walk on the snow.

10. We cannot stop natural disasters, but we can be prepared. People need survival gear. They must set up a plan.

Reading Science

1. All are true about tsunamis and earthquakes **except**–

    A.   both can take place in water.

    B.   both can harm buildings.

    C.   both can be stopped.

    D.   both can harm land.

2. The author organizes this passage by–

    A.   comparing different natural disasters.

    B.   describing natural disasters and telling how humans can stay safe.

    C.   explaining the problem of natural disasters.

    D.   explaining the causes of natural hazards and their effects.

3. Look at the meaning of the word **myth** below.

    Myth\mith\noun
    1. An old story
    2. A made-up person
    3. A made-up story
    4. A false belief

What is the definition of the word **myth** in paragraph 8?

    A.   Definition 1

    B.   Definition 2

    C.   Definition 3

    D.   Definition 4

4. The author most likely wrote this selection to–

    A.   inform readers of differences in natural disasters and how humans can stay safe.

    B.   explain to readers how natural disasters can be stopped.

    C.   try to get readers to make changes that will help stop natural disasters.

    D.   tell readers about a natural disaster.

5. Paragraphs 2 and 3 are mostly about–

    A.   where volcanoes are found on Earth.

    B.   how people can stay safe during a volcanic eruption.

    C.   how volcanoes are unsafe and can harm humans.

    D.   why people should not live close to volcanoes.

6. The reader can tell that park rangers start avalanches–

    A.   to stop avalanches from happening and hurting people.

    B.   to help the snow melt faster.

    C.   to save trees from being damaged.

    D.   to let the snow come down the slope by itself.

Reading Science

7. Which of the following is the best summary of "Amazing Earth"?

A. Natural disasters are unsafe. People should stay away. They need to be safe. Tsunamis are the most dangerous natural disaster. They damage many objects. Earthquakes cause tsunamis.

B. Earth is amazing. We cannot explain the exact reason why there are disasters, but we can do things to help lessen the effects. Humans can have an effect on what happens to our Earth.

C. Sometimes, one disaster can cause another. A volcano can erupt. It causes a tsunami. An earthquake can start a tsunami. An avalanche is unsafe for skiers.

D. Sometimes, nature can be tough. A volcano oozes hot lava onto Earth. Earthquakes harm homes. People should not live near the coast. They should stay away. Avalanches are not safe for hikers. Park rangers start avalanches. People should not live near natural hazards.

8. Read the following sentence from the selection.

Some communities build dikes that help absorb the giant waves.

The reader can tell that a dike is most likely–

A. a large hole in the ground.

B. a large wall built high along the ocean.

C. an area where fish live.

D. a place where people can go for shelter.

∞ **Open-Ended Response**

1. Natural disasters—such as volcanic eruptions, earthquakes, tsunamis, and floods—can change the land and affect humans. What steps can you take to be prepared when these disasters occur?

_____

_____

_____

_____

2. Special pads can be placed in the foundation of a building to allow for movement in the event of a natural disaster. During which event would these pads be the most useful—tsunami, forest fire, or earthquake? Explain.

_____

_____

_____

_____

3. You are an engineer for a company that wants to build homes on a coastline where hurricanes frequently occur. What are some things you must consider before building in this environment?

_____

_____

_____

_____

Claim-Evidence-Reasoning

Scenario:

While humans cannot eliminate natural hazards, they can take steps to reduce the impacts of those hazards. Architects design structures that can withstand the forces of nature, from tsunamis in India to hurricanes in Florida.

External Data:

The following houses have been designed to withstand an earthquake and flooding.

House 1

This house is all concrete and permanently secured to the ground. It is sitting high up on a hill, away from possible flooding.

House 2

This house is shaped like a soccer ball, which reduces any pressure on the walls. It can float, and the base is balanced to help it stay upright.

Prompt:

Which design would best protect the house against earthquakes and flooding, including tsunamis? Use a scientific explanation to justify your answer.

Claim-Evidence-Reasoning

Claim:

_____

_____

_____

_____

Evidence:

_____

_____

_____

_____

_____

_____

Reasoning:

_____

_____

_____

_____

_____

_____

California Instructional Segment

Mission Log

Mission Briefing

Anchoring Phenomena

Where are the impacts of earthquakes the strongest?

Mission Briefing

You are building your first home in California and have to decide where you want to live. Some areas are near fault lines, while others are far away. This determines the cost of the land and the materials that will be used to build the home. How will you decide?

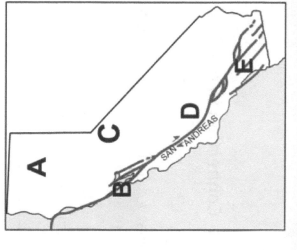

- What do we know about the location and strength of earthquakes?

- How can we describe the amount of shaking in earthquakes?

- How can we minimize the damage from earthquakes?

California Instructional Segment

Mission Log

Class Mission Log

Information Gained

Plate Tectonics

Think back to what you learned before to answer the following question:

How do plate tectonics cause earthquakes?

_____

Natural Processes

Think back to what you learned before to answer the following questions:

What are some natural disasters that occur on Earth?

_____

How does the location on Earth affect the type of natural disasters that occur?

_____

_____

Connection to Mission

Plate Tectonics

Think back to what you learned before to answer the following questions:

What is the name of the plate boundary where the North American and Pacific Plates meet in California?

_____

Draw the way these plates move, using arrows.

Natural Processes

Think back to what you learned before to answer the following question:

What types of structures minimize the damage of earthquakes?

_____

California Instructional Segment

Mission Log

Class Mission Log

Information Gained

Wavelength and Amplitude

What is the difference between wavelength and amplitude?

_____

What is the equipment called that we use to measure waves from earthquakes?

_____

Motion of Waves

How does what the wave travels through affect its motion?

_____

_____

Connection to Mission

Wavelength and Amplitude

How do wavelengths change as they get farther away from the epicenter?

_____

How does the amplitude of waves change as they get farther away from the epicenter?

_____

Motion of Waves

What do we call the waves caused by earthquakes?

_____

_____

California Instructional Segment

Action Plan

Action Plan

You will be getting a budget to spend on your house and property. The budget will also include the materials being used and the preventative structures needed to withstand earthquakes.

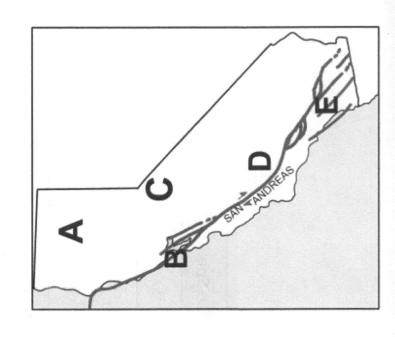

Here's what we know:

- Earthquakes cause damage to land and buildings.

- The effects from earthquake waves can be felt for miles.

- Structure design affects the ability to withstand earthquakes.

- Stronger structures cost more to build.

California Instructional Segment
Action Plan

Take Action

What's my budget?

Roll a die to determine your budget. Remember, this budget has to buy both land and a building!

Number on Die	Amount to Spend
1	$300,000
2	$400,000
3	$500,000
4	$600,000
5	$800,000
6	$900,000

Look at the tables on the next two pages to decide where you will move and what type of house you will own.

California Instructional Segment

Action Plan

Take Action

City	Location Description	Property Cost
A	High in the mountains, lots of trees and sawmills, isolated	$800,000
B	Coastal, near fault line, strong earthquakes, big city	$200,000
C	Flat areas, mild earthquakes, small town	$600,000
D	On fault line, frequent medium-strength earthquakes, midsized town	$400,000
E	Coastal, near several fault lines, large city	$100,000

What is the relationship between the location of the city and the price of the land?

_____

_____

Explain why this relationship exists.

_____

_____

California Instructional Segment

Action Plan

Cost of House	Type of House
$100,000	Extra-small house
$600,000	Large house
$200,000	Small house
$400,000	Medium house
$800,000	Extra-large house

What is the relationship between the cost of the house and the type of house?

Earthquake protection packages are available for each house. There are three levels of protection offered.

Level 1 (least protection)	$100,000
Level 2 (medium protection)	$200,000
Level 3 (highest protection)	$300,000

California Instructional Segment

Action Plan

Take Action

Total budget:

Location picked and cost:

Home size and cost:

Earthquake protection and cost:

Total spent:

What is the relationship between the location you chose and the size of the house you could build?

_____

_____

Are there any risks involved with your location? How could these be overcome?

_____

_____

Which level of earthquake protection did you buy? Why?

_____

_____

Wavelength and Amplitude

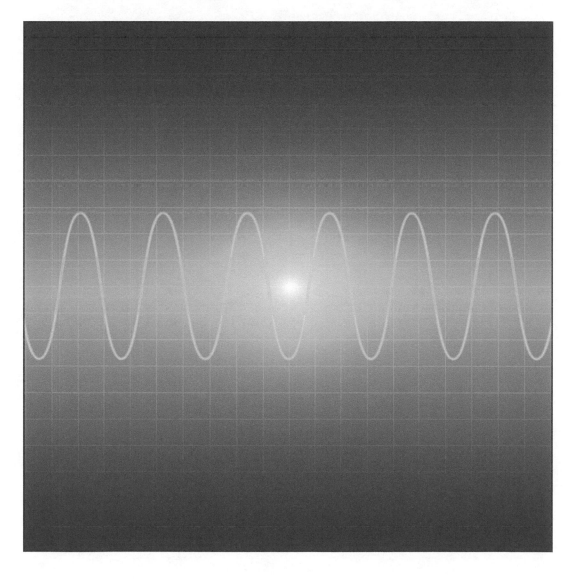

Name: _____

Date: _____

Graphic Organizer

Wavelength and Amplitude

Directions

Identify and write "wavelength" and "amplitude" on the wave below. Then draw waves with different wavelengths and amplitudes and describe how they affect the motion of an object.

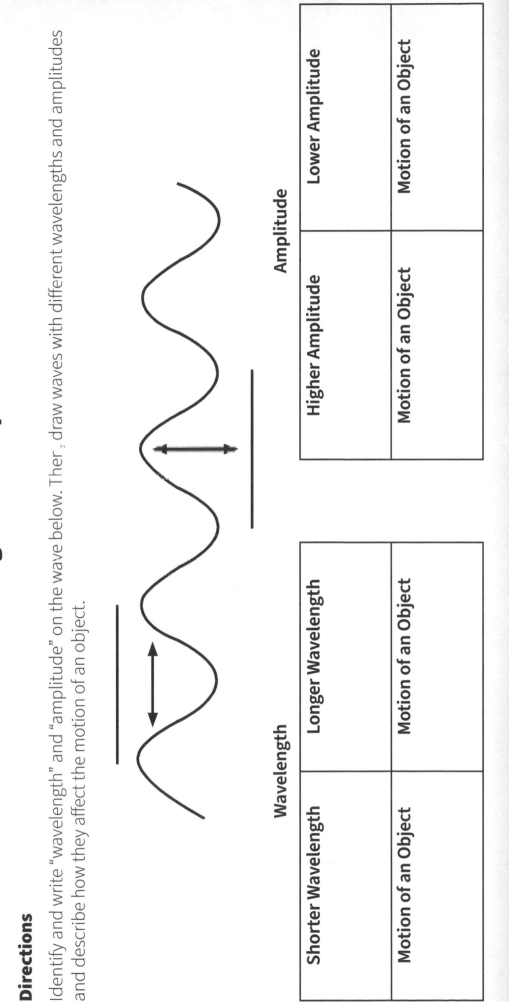

Wavelength

Shorter Wavelength	Longer Wavelength
Motion of an Object	Motion of an Object

Amplitude

Higher Amplitude	Lower Amplitude
Motion of an Object	Motion of an Object

Explore 1

Wave Challenge

Part I

1. Drawing of a **Slow** Rope Flick

[ ]

2. Drawing of a **Quick** Rope Flick

[ ]

From one peak to the next is called the wavelength, and the height from midway between the highest and lowest points is called the amplitude. Label the wavelength and the amplitude on each of your drawings.

Explore 1

Part II

1. Drawing of a Wave with a **Large** Amplitude

2. Drawing of a Wave with a **Small** Amplitude

3. Drawing of a Wave with **Short** Wavelengths

4. Drawing of a Wave with **Long** Wavelengths

Explore 1

1. What did these waves have in common?

_____

_____

_____

_____

2. What was different about these waves?

_____

_____

_____

_____

3. Did you notice any patterns that occurred when making waves?

_____

_____

_____

_____

Explore 1

Wave Challenge

Claim-Evidence-Reasoning

Write a scientific explanation for what wave conditions you think would be the most difficult to drive through in a boat. Make sure you use the words amplitude and wavelength in your reasoning.

Claim:

_____

_____

_____

Evidence:

_____

_____

_____

_____

Reasoning:

_____

_____

_____

_____

_____

_____

🔍 Explore 2

Waves and Motion

Our Driving Question:

How do wavelength and amplitude affect the motion of objects?

What We Need:

1 Clear, plastic tub
1 Plastic cup
1 Dry-erase marker
1 Stopwatch
Water
1 Balloon
1 Ruler

Procedure:

Part I

1. One group member should use the dry-erase marker to draw where the waterline is on the clear tub.

2. One group member will hold the cup at one end of the tub. Push the cup into the water to make the following four types of waves:

   a. Long wavelength with low amplitude

   b. Short wavelength with low amplitude

   c. Long wavelength with high amplitude

   d. Short wavelength with high amplitude

3. Record your observations from step 2 and answer the reflection questions.

Explore 2

Part II

1. Your group will be repeating the Part I investigation, except now you will place a blown-up balloon at one end of the clear tub, opposite the end where the cup is manipulating the water.

2. One group member should use the dry-erase marker to draw where the waterline is on the clear tub.

3. One group member will hold the cup at one end of the tub. The group member will push the cup into the water to make the following four types of waves:

   a. Long wavelength with low amplitude

   b. Short wavelength with low amplitude

   c. Long wavelength with high amplitude

   d. Short wavelength with high amplitude

4. One group member will start the stopwatch when the other group member begins manipulating the water with the cup to make the various waves.

5. Another group member will use the dry-erase marker to make a quick mark on the clear tub to indicate how high the balloon goes when a wave moves it up.

6. The remaining group members will count how many times the balloon goes up and down in 15 seconds. At the end of the 15 seconds, use a ruler to see how high the balloon moved up.

7. Record this information and how many times the balloon went up and down in 15 seconds and answer the reflection questions.

Explore 2

Part I Data and Reflection Questions:

Wave Characteristics	Draw What Each Wave Looked Like
Long wavelength, low amplitude	
Short wavelength, low amplitude	
Long wavelength, high amplitude	
Short wavelength, high amplitude	

1. How did you change the wavelength of your waves?

_____

_____

2. How did you change the amplitude of your waves?

_____

3. Describe the wavelength of the fastest waves.

_____

4. Describe the wavelength of the slowest waves.

_____

5. Describe the amplitude of the tallest waves.

_____

6. Describe the amplitude of the shortest waves.

_____

Explore 2

Part II Data and Reflection Questions:

Wave Characteristics	Number of Times Balloon Moved Up and Down in 15 Seconds	How High Did the Balloon Move Up?
Long wavelength, low amplitude		_____ cm
Short wavelength, low amplitude		_____ cm
Long wavelength, high amplitude		_____ cm
Short wavelength, high amplitude		_____ cm

1. What caused the balloon to move up in the water the most?

_____

2. What caused the balloon to move up in the water the least?

_____

3. Describe the wavelength and amplitude needed to make the balloon go up and down the greatest number of times.

_____

_____

4. Describe the wavelength and amplitude needed to make the balloon go up and down the least number of times.

_____

_____

🔍 Explore 3

Waves in the Earth

The Problem

When an earthquake occurs, waves travel through Earth's crust. These waves cause the crust to move. You have learned that waves have amplitude and wavelength. When an earthquake wave has a higher amplitude and shorter wavelength, there will be a lot of motion in Earth's crust. When an earthquake wave has lower amplitude and longer wavelength, there will be less motion in Earth's crust. You live in an area that is prone to earthquakes, and you want to keep a record of earthquakes by finding a way to record their amplitudes and wavelengths. Current seismographs are too expensive to buy.

The Challenge

Create an affordable seismograph that will record an earthquake's amplitude and wavelength.

Criteria and Constraints

- Create a blueprint of your seismograph.

- Only the materials provided may be used.

- All changes to the design must be included on the blueprint.

- The structure should be able to record amplitude and wavelength when a desk is lightly shaken for 10 seconds.

Brainstorm and Research

Write down any ideas you have about how you could master the challenge. If you need more information, write down what you need to know and gain permission from your teacher to research the answer.

Explore 3

Design Plan

Use the ideas you wrote down while brainstorming to develop a final design plan. Draw your plan and label the parts. Be sure to list what each part is made of.

Build and Test

Build your design and test it. Does it meet all the criteria and constraints? Use the space below to list what problems you need to fix in your design.

Refine and Redesign

How could you solve the problems you found during testing? Use the space below to draw a new design that should solve the problems.

Explore 3

Retest and Finalize

Build and test your new design. Does it meet all the criteria and constraints? If not, repeat the refine and redesign process. If so, move on to planning your presentation.

Presentation Plan

Use the space below to plan how you will present your final product. Be sure to include who will speak and what you want to say. Your presentation should include the scientific ideas used to solve this design challenge.

![Linking Literacy logo] **Linking Literacy**
During-Reading

Wavelength and Amplitude

Main Ideas and Details

While you read: Look for details that give more information about the two main ideas listed below. Write four details for every main idea.

Text Topic: **Waves travel through material as vibrations and transmit energy.**

Page	Main Idea:	Detail 1	Detail 2
	Waves can be compared by the way they behave.	Detail 3	Detail 4

Linking Literacy
During-Reading

Page	Main Idea:	Detail 1	Detail 2
	Waves have different characteristics.	Detail 3	Detail 4

Draw a picture to demonstrate your understanding of wavelength and amplitude.

Wavelength

Amplitude

Linking Literacy
Post-Reading

Comparing Waves

Directions: Think of all the characteristics of waves you read about. Look at the waves below, and label the waves that have the highest and lowest amplitudes and the longest and shortest wavelengths.

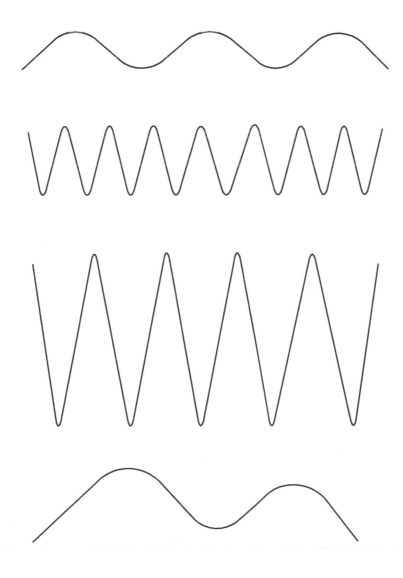

📖 Reading Science

Waves All Around

1. Waves are all around us. They are everywhere, and we can't even see many of them. We see them in the ocean when the wind or storm creates them. We see surfers riding on them. However, there are many more kinds of waves than just ocean waves. Waves help us use a microwave to cook food. They help us see pictures of the inside of our bodies, using X-ray technology. Waves help our senses know the world around us.

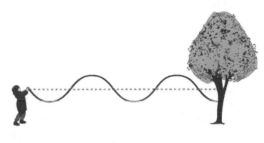

2. Waves are always moving. Waves have energy. Energy keeps waves moving, but magnetism holds them together. Magnetism is the power to be attracted to something. Magnetism does not allow waves to break up. No matter what a wave is made of, its matter stays together because of magnetism.

3. The eye sees light and color in waves. We can't physically see the wave moving, but it's there. When we measure color, it travels as waves of energy. Different colors of light have different wavelengths. A wavelength is the distance between one wave and the next wave. Purple and blue have short, fast waves. Red has a longer, bigger wave. The difference between these colors' waves is exactly why we see different colors. Every color in the rainbow has its own unique wave speed and size that make it stand out from other colors. If there were no color waves, we would see everything as dark or dim.

4. Another sense that uses waves is hearing. Sound creates tiny vibrations in the air around us. The vibrations travel through the air as a sound wave. A foghorn is a low-pitched sound. The wave travels slowly. A whistle is a high-pitched sound. The wave travels quickly. In high-pitched sounds, many waves occur per second.

5. We hear the volume of sound by measuring the amplitude of the sound wave. The amplitude is the height of the wave measured from its middle position. When the TV at your house is loud, the wave's amplitude is high. When it is quiet, the wave's amplitude is low. Volume is related to the pressure of the air particles that bump into each other when a sound is made. Without the movement of air around us, we would hear nothing. The Moon has no air. Therefore, it's silent on the Moon.

6. Aside from our senses, scientists use waves to measure changes in Earth. These waves are called seismic waves. Seismic waves are elastic waves. They cause brief distortions of solid materials. Scientists use seismographs to record these changes. Seismographs are tools used to measure sound waves within Earth. They allow scientists to hear sounds caused by changes that are going on within Earth hundreds of miles away. Instead of guessing where events might occur, scientists can use the seismograph to record sound waves that will allow the scientists to keep track of the changes. Scientists don't have warning systems for earthquakes. They are still working on designing a system.

7. Waves are important in our everyday lives. They help us see and hear the world around us. With the help of waves, humans are able to experience the beauty of Earth. Scientists also need waves to help them learn more about changes that happen within Earth. Without the different kinds of waves, life would be silent, colorless, and dangerous. Who knew our world was so minute that each sound we hear or color we see is its own individual wave? That is pretty remarkable!

# Reading Science

1. Paragraph 3 is mostly about–

A. how the human eye sees light.

B. how the human eye sees color.

C. how each color has its own unique wave.

D. how different colors of light have different wavelengths.

2. What evidence helps the reader know the meaning of **distortions** in paragraph 6?

A. *Seismograph*

B. *Solid materials*

C. *Record*

D. *Changes*

Reading Science

3. How are sound and color waves similar?

    A.   Each color has its own wave, just like each sound has its own wave.

    B.   Color waves and sound waves are the same size.

    C.   Color waves and sound waves are both long waves.

    D.   Sound waves and color waves are not similar.

4. "Waves All Around" is mostly about–

    A.   how our eyes and ears need waves to live.

    B.   how the human eye physically cannot see waves.

    C.   how seismic waves help predict future earthquakes.

    D.   how the measurement of waves helps us know more about the world around us.

Reading Science

5. To help the reader better understand the passage, the author organizes the passage–

    A   by listing the cause of waves and how they affect our lives.

    B.   by comparing and contrasting different types of waves and explaining why we need them.

    C.   by describing different types of waves and how they benefit human life.

    D.   by sequencing the events of how the human eye and ear use waves to see and hear.

6. The reader can infer that people who are color-blind–

    A.   do not see certain color waves.

    B.   see all color waves.

    C.   see only in black and white.

    D.   see color waves that are longer or shorter than what a non-color-blind eye sees.

Reading Science

7. The author most likely wrote this passage to–

   A.   explain how color gets to the human eye.

   B.   talk about the differences between waves and explain why people need them.

   C.   inform the reader of how important waves are in everyday life.

   D.   explain to the reader how to understand a wave's length and height.

∞ **Open-Ended Response**

1. Write your own definition of the word *amplitude* and give an example.

_____

_____

_____

_____

2. The difference between *wavelength* and *amplitude* is . . .

_____

_____

_____

_____

3. Your teacher drops a stone into a container of water. Describe what you observe in this demonstration. Use the words wavelength and amplitude to explain the movement of the water.

_____

_____

_____

_____

Claim-Evidence-Reasoning

Wavelength and Amplitude

Scenario:

Elizabeth was watching the news about an earthquake that had occurred in California. On the news, she saw the following picture and decided to start a collection at school to help the children in a highly affected area. Elizabeth wants to send the donations to the city that most likely received the most damage. Each line on the map below shows a peak of the waves sent out by the earthquake, and the center of the circles is the epicenter. The thicker the line, the higher the amplitude.

Prompt:

Using scientific reasoning, explain which of the cities on the map Elizabeth should send her donations to.

Claim:

_____

_____

_____

_____

_____

Claim-Evidence-Reasoning

Evidence:

_____
_____
_____
_____
_____
_____
_____

Reasoning:

_____
_____
_____
_____
_____
_____
_____
_____
_____
_____
_____
_____
_____

Motion of Waves

Name: _____   Date: _____

Graphic Organizer

All About Waves

Directions

Fill in the concept map with information about waves.

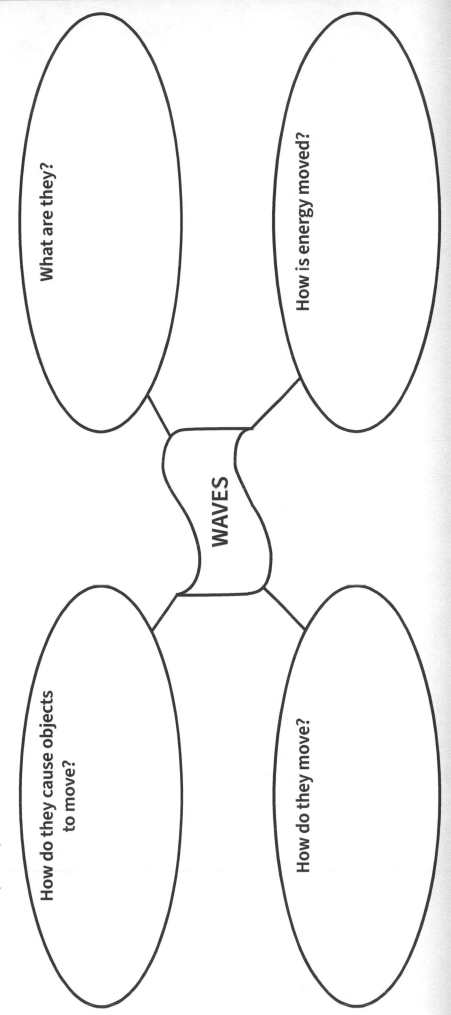

What are they?

How is energy moved?

WAVES

How do they cause objects to move?

How do they move?

Explore 1

Disturbing Water

Part I

Record your observations as you drop water onto the surface of the water in the pan. Draw an illustration of what happens on the surface of the water.

```
[blank box for illustration]
```

1. What happened when you dropped water into the pan?

_____

2. Describe the pattern of motion created by the waves.

_____

_____

3. Use arrows to label the direction(s) of your waves in your drawing above.

4. Where were the waves the biggest? Where were they the smallest?

_____

_____

5. How is this model similar to waves in the ocean?

_____

_____

_____

Explore 1

Part II

Illustrate your model with the glitter and write down your observations in the space below.

1. What direction did the clump of glitter move?

_____

2. Did the clump of glitter move to the edge of the pan?

_____

3. What does this model tell you about waves moving objects out in the ocean?

_____

_____

_____

Explore 1

Disturbing Water

Claim-Evidence-Reasoning

Write a scientific explanation for how waves affect the motion of other objects. Make a claim and state your evidence and reasoning.

Claim:

_____

_____

_____

_____

Evidence:

_____

_____

_____

_____

Reasoning:

_____

_____

_____

_____

Linking Literacy
During-Reading

Nuts and Bolts

While you read: Write down the important ideas. Then create a summary by using the important ideas.

Important Ideas

- _____
  _____
- _____
  _____
- _____
  _____
- _____
  _____
- _____
  _____

Summary: Write a summary of the text in your own words.

_____
_____
_____
_____
_____
_____
_____

Linking Literacy
Post-Reading

Name: _____ Date: _____

Wave Concepts

After you read: Write about the motions of waves that you read about in the STEMscopedia. List four facts that you learned about the subject. Additional bubbles can be drawn in, if necessary.

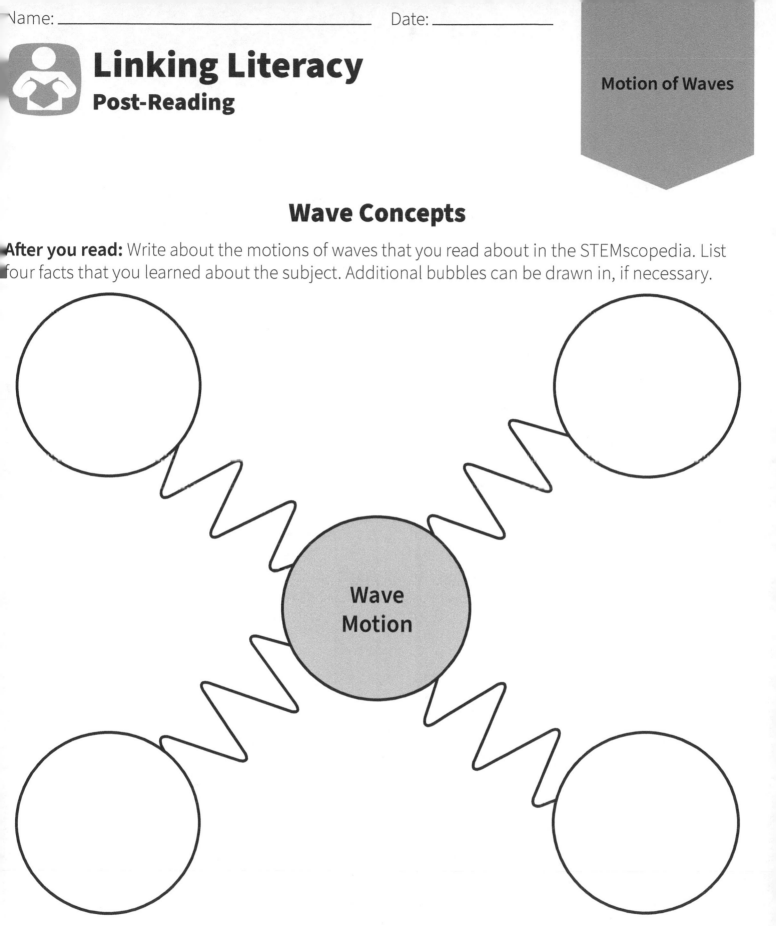

Reading Science

Making Waves

1. Nathan and Brant sat in front of their TV, playing video games. Because they'd spent most of their summer days in front of the TV, their mom decided it was time for them to stop wasting away their summer. "Boys, it's time to go enjoy nature. It is a beautiful summer day. The weather is wonderful! Turn off your video games and go play outside."

2. "But there's nothing to do outside," complained Brant as he put down his game controller.

3. Agreeing with his brother while shutting off the television, Nathan argued, "It's boring outside. There's nothing to do, Mom."

4. Their mom had an idea. "Why don't you gather your fishing poles and go on a pond adventure? I bought some bait at the store this morning. I placed it in the garage."

5. Realizing they hadn't been fishing all summer, Nathan and Brant looked at each other and shrugged their shoulders. They decided to take their mom's advice and headed to the garage to gather their fishing gear. They collected their tackle box, fishing poles, and bait. After their mom handed them a small cooler packed with drinks and snacks, the two boys were on their way to their fishing adventure.

6. "Let's see who can catch the most fish!" declared Brant on their walk to the pond.

7. "Game on! I'm the world's best angler!" exclaimed Nathan as his eyes beamed like the glow of a full Moon.

8. The boys arrived at the small pond. They **configured** their poles by putting on a bobber, a small hook, and some bait. Their fishing lines whizzed through the air and landed softly in the calm water as the boys planted themselves on the beach. Their bobbers sat afloat while they watched closely, waiting patiently for a fish to take the bait.

9. Minutes passed, which seemed like hours. The boys became discouraged, as the fishing conditions were unfavorable. Nathan and Brant began believing they were running out of fisherman's luck.

10. Before long, Nathan picked up a small pebble and threw it into the water. He watched as his fishing bobber moved up and down very calmly. He noticed the water swelled toward the beach, but the bobber stayed put.

11. "Brant, why don't you think my bobber moved forward? The water moved when I threw that pebble, but the bobber didn't," said Nathan.

12. "What are you talking about?" asked Brant, confused.

13. "Watch this," said Nathan as he selected another small pebble and threw it into the pond. The boys watched as a circle appeared around the area where the pebble had landed. The water seemed to move toward them, but the bobber stayed in the exact same spot.

14. "That's so unusual," said Nathan. "Because the water came to the beach, I thought the bobber would have also moved closer. I wonder what would happen if we were to try it with a bigger rock. Maybe that will move the bobber closer to shore."

15. The now-inquisitive boys looked for bigger stones to throw in the water. They **scavenged** around the pond until they had a couple of different-sized stones. Picking up a larger stone, Brant chucked it into the water. The boys watched as the water waved toward the beach. Water came up to their toes, but the bobber did not budge.

16. "Try a bigger one," suggested Nathan.

17. Brant chose a larger stone than before and pitched it into the water. Larger waves came to the beach this time, covering the boys' feet. Again, the bobber did not shift.

18. "I'll try throwing the next one with more muscle. If I put some force on my throw, maybe it will create a bigger wave and bring the bobber to the beach," predicted Nathan. He picked up the largest stone the boys had collected and heaved it into the water with all his might. The waves gushed to the beach, eventually ceasing.

19. "Wow, those were some sizable waves," exclaimed Brant. "Why isn't the bobber moving, though? I thought waves carried water forward."

20. "Well, it doesn't look like that is true," responded Nathan. "Maybe waves don't really move water. I think they are a motion that happens through water. They only cause the water to move up and down in place. The water never really leaves its original place in the pond. When the water reaches the beach, it pushes forward, because it has no other water to bring it back down."

21. Brant thought for a moment. "That explains why the bobber stays in the same spot. I think we just conducted a scientific investigation!"

22. Brant smiled as Nathan's mouth formed a grin. "We are some incredible scientists!"

23. Brant pointed to the pond and shrieked, "Quick! Grab your line! Your bobber is moving without us throwing a stone! You have a bite!"

24. Running as fast as lightning strikes to his fishing pole, Nathan arrived just in time to reel in his mighty catch. Bringing his hook to shore and closer to his eyesight, he saw a tiny minnow attached. "Though he's petite, I still beat you in the fish catch, and that makes me reign supreme as world's best angler!" boasted Nathan.

25. "The day is not over yet," thought Brant as he continued to laugh about his brother's minute catch of the day.

Reading Science

1. Which word in paragraph 8 helps the reader figure out the meaning of the word **configured?**

    A. *Whizzed*

    B. *Putting*

    C. *Bobber*

    D. *Bait*

2. Why is it important to the story that the fishing conditions were unfavorable?

    A. The boys conducted a science investigation with rocks and learned about waves.

    B. The boys had to find another activity to keep them occupied at the pond.

    C. The boys had to learn to be patient.

    D. The boys got out of the house on the beautiful day and went to the pond.

Reading Science

3. What does the word **scavenged** mean in paragraph 15?

    A.   Ignored

    B.   Neglected

    C.   Stared

    D.   Prowled

4. Which sentence supports the idea that waves do not push water forward but instead move water up and down in the same place?

    A.   *The boys watched as a circle appeared around the area where the pebble had landed.*

    B.   *"Maybe some force will create a larger wave. Maybe the bobber will come to the beach."*

    C.   *"Your bobber is moving without us throwing a stone!"*

    D.   *"I'll try throwing the next one with more muscle. Maybe some force will create a larger wave."*

Reading Science

5. The reader can assume the boys were feeling–

    A.   discouraged after they caught a tiny minnow.

    B.   encouraged by throwing stones into the pond.

    C.   annoyed that their mom made them shut off their video games.

    D.   fatigued from being at the pond.

6. What is the best summary of the selection?

    A.   Two brothers are spending too much time playing video games, so their mom makes them shut the TV off. She suggests they go fishing. The boys go to the pond and throw rocks into the water to watch the waves. The bigger the rocks they throw, the bigger the waves that are formed.

    B.   Nathan and Brant get ready to go fishing at the pond. They gather up all their supplies and head to the pond, where they don't catch many fish. They conduct a science experiment on the motion of waves while they are there.

    C.   Nathan and Brant are fishing at the pond. Nathan throws a rock in the pond and notices that the water moves to the beach but his bobber does not. Curious to find out why, he and Brant gather larger rocks and try different approaches to see if they can get the bobber to move closer to the beach.

    D.   Two boys are wasting away their summer days until their mom suggests they go fishing. They reluctantly go. They don't have much luck fishing, so they begin throwing stones in the water. They notice the water comes to the beach, but their bobber does not move. As they try different ways to get the bobber to move, they end up learning about waves.

Reading Science

7. Why do the boys search for larger stones?

    A.   They believe they won't have to throw them as hard.

    B.   They believe larger stones will create more force in the water, bringing the bobber to the beach.

    C.   They believe the larger stones will be easier to see.

    D.   They believe the larger stones will create larger circles as they land in the water.

Name: _____ Date: _____

∞ Open-Ended Response

Short Answer:

1. How is the water moving in the picture?

_____

_____

_____

_____

2. How does water move in the deep ocean? How does the water move when waves meet the beach?

_____

_____

_____

_____

3. Imagine you are floating on a boat out in the deep ocean. Do the waves carry you back to the beach? Why or why not?

_____

_____

_____

_____

Claim-Evidence-Reasoning

Motion of Waves

Scenario:

Kim and Elizabeth are out on a deep-sea fishing trip. Off in the distance, they see a floating buoy. There are some large waves out there, and they wonder if the waves will make the buoy float toward their boat so they can get a better look.

Prompt:

Write a scientific explanation describing if the buoy will move closer to Kate and Elizabeth.

Claim:

_____

_____

_____

_____

_____

_____

_____

Claim-Evidence-Reasoning

Evidence:

_____

_____

_____

_____

_____

_____

_____

_____

Reasoning:

_____

_____

_____

_____

_____

_____

_____

_____

_____

_____

_____

_____

_____

_____

California Instructional Segment

Mission Log

Mission Briefing

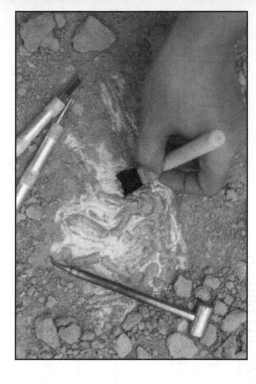

Anchoring Phenomena

How can we use fossils to help determine the physical characteristics of extinct animals and the environments they lived in?

Mission Briefing

You work for a science museum and study fossils. Paleontologists have discovered a skeleton in the desert. They are unable to identify this animal because it is a new discovery. You are asked to determine what this animal could have looked like and how it lived.

- What external structures would this animal have needed to survive?

- How could this animal have communicated?

California Instructional Segment

Mission Log

Class Mission Log

Information Gained

Transfer of Energy in Collision

Think back to what you learned before to answer the following question:

How does sound energy travel?

_____

_____

Sense Receptors

What are some ways that animals use their senses to respond to their environment?

_____

_____

_____

Connection to Mission

Transfer of Energy in Collision

Think back to what you learned before to answer the following question:

How do desert animals transfer sound energy back and forth to each other?

_____

_____

Sense Receptors

List ways desert animals might communicate with others of its kind.

_____

Describe how some desert animals warn others of its kind of impending danger.

_____

What type of communication could a desert animal use to scare away possible predators?

_____

California Instructional Segment

Mission Log

Class Mission Log

Information Gained

Connection to Mission

Plant and Animal Parts

Plant and Animal Parts

How do an animal's body parts help it survive?

Some structures and behaviors help animals survive in the desert. Read the examples below and describe how each structure or behavior could help an animal survive.

_____

_____

- Body retaining water:

- Being nocturnal:

What can we learn about an animal by observing its body parts?

- Large eyes:

- Large ears:

_____

- Burrowing:

_____

- Being an herbivore:

_____

_____

California Instructional Segment

Mission Log

Class Mission Log

Information Gained

Connection to Mission

Light Reflection

Light Reflection

What role does light play in how we see?

How are the eyes of desert animals adapted to their environment?

Do all animals have the same type of vision?

How might eyes differ between predator and prey?

Information Technologies

Information Technologies

Why is it important for animals to be able to communicate?

What are some ways that desert animals communicate with each other

![California Instructional Segment logo]

California Instructional Segment
Action Plan

Action Plan

Predict what an animal may have looked like based on the environment in which it lived.

Here's what we know

- The rock layer in which the fossil was found indicates a desert environment.

- The animal's fossil shows that it was nocturnal.

- The animal's fossil indicates that it was a plant eater.

- The fossil had evidence that it burrowed during the day.

- Animals can use energy to communicate.

California Instructional Segment

Action Plan

Take Action

The new fossil was found in a rock layer that indicates a desert environment. You have been asked to help determine what the animal may have looked like when it was living.

List the characteristics of a desert environment.

_____

_____

_____

What external structures help animals survive in the desert?

_____

_____

_____

_____

California Instructional Segment

Action Plan

Take Action

Draw what you think this animal could have looked like while alive in its environment. Describe how it communicated with others.

Sense Receptors

Name: _____ Date: _____

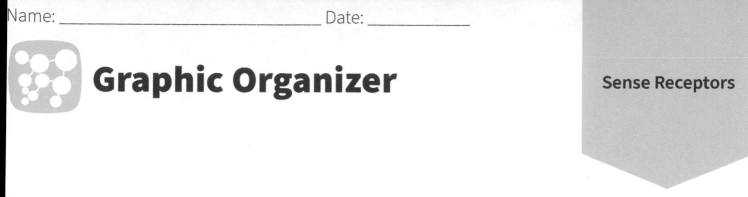

Graphic Organizer

Makes Sense!

Directions

Sense receptors pick up information from an animal's environment and send it to the brain. The brain then tells the animal how it should react. Choose an animal. In the *Information Receiver* column, write and underline the sense organ your animal is using. Then write one example of a situation your animal might encounter in its environment through its sense receptors. In the *Information Response* column, write how your animal's brain might tell it to react.

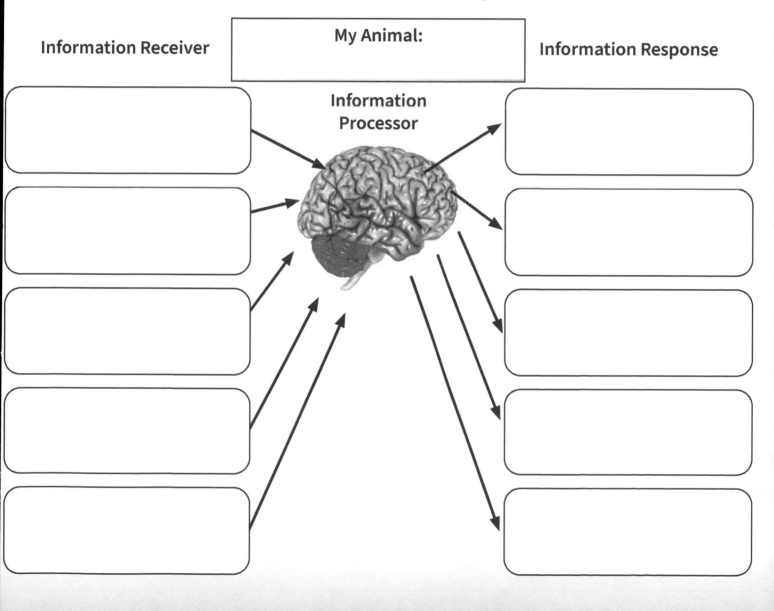

Information Receiver

My Animal:

Information Response

Information Processor

Name: _____ Date: _____

Hook

What's That Smell?

Write what scent you think is inside each canister, what it reminds you of, and what the actual scent is.

My Guess	Reminds Me Of . . .	Actual
1.		
2.		
3.		
4.		
5.		
6.		

Did any of the scents make you want to do something or act in a certain way? Explain how.

_____

_____

_____

_____

_____

_____

_____

_____

Explore 1

Reactive Senses

Meerkats use a wide range of sounds to communicate with each other. Some of the sounds have been deciphered and are listed below.

Sound	Meaning
purr	to show contentment or attachment to another meerkat
chatter	to show nervousness
squeal	to alert others to danger
dominant male or female call	to show it's time to hunt
lookout cry of alarm	to signal a predator on land
lookout yelp	to signal a predator in the air

Work in your groups to come up with two types of calls. One call should signal safety, and the other should signal danger. List your signals below.

Safety Signal: _____   Danger Signal: _____

What happened to the students who couldn't remember or hear their signals?

_____

If other meerkats' signals were different than yours, how would it make communicating with your group more difficult?

_____

_____

_____

What sense receptors did your meerkat gang use to protect itself?

_____

What role did your brain play in protecting you?

_____

_____

Explore 1

Reactive Senses

Claim-Evidence-Reasoning

Use the information you gathered during the activity to complete the following task.

Write a scientific explanation that describes the importance of communication between animals like the meerkat. Make a claim, and state your evidence and reasoning.

Claim:

_____

_____

_____

Evidence:

_____

_____

_____

_____

Reasoning:

_____

_____

_____

_____

_____

_____

Explore 2

Sensing Danger

The Problem

Zoologists have just heard about a new animal species on a remote island. They have very little information about the animal, and they have not yet been able to determine how the animal senses and responds to danger. They do know that animals use specialized sense receptors to sense danger and different methods to respond to danger. Some known examples of how animals respond to danger are listed below.

Animal	Response to Sensing Danger
squid	squirts ink to disorient the predator as it gets away
putter fish	puffs up to look bigger and more intimidating
porcupine	has spines all over its body to keep predators away
cat	hisses to keep others away

Because of your outstanding work in science class, you are given the opportunity to be the first "junior zoologist" to visit the island and learn about this new species, on the condition that you inform other zoologists about this amazing animal on your return.

The Challenge

Make a labeled drawing and a model of the new species of animal using the materials provided. The animal will need to have a way of sensing and responding to danger.

Explore 2

Criteria and Constraints

- You must make and label a drawing of your new animal species.

- The drawing must identify how your animal senses danger and how it will respond to that danger.

- The animal's sense receptor or receptors should be designed to increase the sense or senses (ex: large, cupped ears would increase hearing).

- You should create a model of your animal species that includes the appropriate sense receptors and method of responding to danger.

- The animal model must not be any larger than 30 cm high, 30 cm wide, and 30 cm long.

Brainstorm and Research

Write down any ideas you have about how you could master the challenge. If you need more information, write down what you need to know and gain permission from your teacher to research the answer.

Explore 2

Design Plan

Use the ideas you wrote down while brainstorming to develop a final design plan. Draw your plan and label the parts. Be sure to list what each part is made of.

Build and Test

Build your design and test it. Does it meet all the criteria and constraints? Use the space below to list what problems you need to fix in your design.

Refine and Redesign

How could you solve the problems you found during testing? Use the space below to draw your new design that should solve the problems.

Retest and Finalize

Build and test your new design. Does it meet all the criteria and constraints? If not, repeat the refine and redesign process. If so, move on to plan your presentation.

Presentation Plan

Use the space below to plan how you will present your final product. Be sure to include who will speak and what you want to say. Your presentation should include the scientific ideas used to solve this design challenge.

Name: _____ Date: _____

Linking Literacy
Pre- and During-Reading

Previewing Vocabulary

Group Directions:

1. Independently skim the text and highlight any vocabulary words you don't know or understand.

2. Fill out the table by adding highlighted words to the *Unknown Word* column. Evaluate your own understanding of the word by placing a check mark under the appropriate column: *I Know It, Have Heard or Seen It*, or *No Clue*.

3. Attempt to define the word, using your collective knowledge and context clues from the text. You may use a dictionary to define words you do not know. When your group is all done, share your definitions with your group.

Unknown Word	Pre-Reading			During-Reading
	I Know It	Have Heard or Seen It	No Clue	Definition

Linking Literacy
Pre- and During-Reading

| Unknown Word | Pre-Reading | | During-Reading |
	I Know It	Have Heard or Seen It	No Clue	Definition

Linking Literacy
Post-Reading

Draw and Explain

After reading: Write a definition for each word in your own words. Then, draw a picture.

	Your Definition	Your Picture
Thermoreceptors		
Chemoreceptors		
Electroreceptors		
Nociceptors		

Draw and label a picture of an animal that uses one of the sensory receptors you have learned about in the text. Explain how it helps the animal on the lines below.

In this picture . . .

_____

_____

_____

_____

Reading Science

A Visit to the Zoo

1. "Dad, can we please go?" begged Jamie.

2. "How are you going to stay up that late?" asked Jamie's dad.

3. "I'll take a nap. I promise!" replied Jamie.

4. "Okay, if you promise to take a nap, we can go," agreed her dad.

5. "Woo-hoo!" screamed Jamie as she ran through the house, jumping about.

6. Jamie was an animal expert in her classroom. If someone wanted to know about an animal, they would ask Jamie. She had recently finished her research project on the life of a veterinarian. In fact, she wanted to be a veterinarian or zoologist when she got older. She had been begging her dad for weeks to take her to the zoo for the Nocturnal Nights exhibit so she could learn more about animals that are awake at night. She was beside herself that her dad had finally agreed.

7. The day of the event arrived, and Jamie did as she promised, even though she was a little excited. After dinner, Jamie and her dad hopped in the car and set off for the zoo.

8. "I can't wait to get there! I wonder what animals we will learn about!" exclaimed Jamie as her dad drove the car closer to the zoo.

9. When they arrived, Jamie hopped out of the car and began walking quickly toward the zoo entrance.

10. "Wait for me!" called her dad as he ran to catch up.

11. After getting checked in, Jamie and her dad met Ben, who announced that he would be their zoo guide for the evening. The three proceeded to put on headlamps so they could see in the dark. Ben explained that it was important to be quiet as they **strode** through the zoo. This was important to really experience nocturnal animals in action.

12. Ben first led them to the owl cage. As soon as they arrived, Jamie was **bug-eyed**. She saw the spotted owl. She had never seen an owl at work at night. Jamie knew that owls are nocturnal and they do most of their hunting at night, but her curiosity wanted to know more.

13. "How are they able to see at night?" whispered Jamie.

14. "Owls have an incredible sense of sight," Ben quietly responded. "Their eyes see two to three times better than humans' eyes. This is because their eyes are long tubes, whereas human eyes are like balls. Owls can't roll their eyes like humans, which is why their heads are able to turn almost all the way around. The owl's wide face allows it to have a wider vision span, giving it binocular-like vision."

15. "Wow! So, is that how they are able to hunt so well at night?" asked Jamie.

16. "Well, they also have a great sense of hearing. Did you know an owl can hear a mouse move? A tiny, little mouse! Isn't that incredible? There is no doubt they have some of the best hearing of any animal. Their ears are funnel-shaped to absorb sound better. An owl can also quietly sneak up on its prey. Their fluffy, thick feathers give them almost silent flight," informed Ben.

17. "Can owls taste? Do they remember that a mouse tastes good?" inquired Jamie.

18. "An owl's sense of taste and touch are not as good as their eyesight and hearing. When an owl is learning to hunt, it remembers sounds that help it catch prey throughout the rest of its life," answered Ben.

19. "You sure know so much about owls," whispered Jamie.

20. "They are very interesting creatures," replied Ben.

21. The three continued through the zoo. Jamie was filled with other questions about animals' senses. Ben informed her by the tiger exhibit that cats grow whiskers as wide as their bodies. The whiskers help them know whether they will fit through spaces. Cats use their sense of perception by using the feeling in their whiskers. If their whiskers clear a space, they know their body will, too. Jamie was also informed about how a porcupine sticks up its quills because it has a strong sense of smell. Ben explained that when a porcupine smells any new or different smell, it sticks up its quills to protect itself.

22. Jamie loved this new information. She couldn't stop smiling. She was thinking about what she was going to share with her friends. The final stop on the Nocturnal Nights zoo tour was the red panda's cage. Jamie was surprised to find out that the red panda was nocturnal.

23. "How does the red panda use its senses to be awake at night?" asked Jamie.

24. "Unlike the owl, the red panda does not have the greatest hearing or eyesight. However, it is an excellent tree climber and can find most of its diet, consisting of bamboo leaves, fruit, and occasionally insects, in the trees. The red panda uses its sense of taste to make sure it finds the proper food. They are not predators, like the owl or cat, so they use their senses in a different way," explained Ben.

25. "Learning about all these nocturnal animals was so much fun," exclaimed Jamie as she stared off into the distance. "Thank you for teaching me, Ben!"

26. "You are very welcome," Ben responded. "Do you have any more questions for me?"

27. "Not for you, but I do have one question for my dad. Can we go home? This was fun, but I'm tired," Jamie said as she yawned.

28. As Ben and her dad chuckled, Jamie sat down on a nearby bench and closed her eyes.

29. "I better get this girl, who is definitely not nocturnal, home to her bed. Thanks for the tour, Ben. We learned so much and had fun with you," thanked Jamie's dad.

30. Ben and her dad shook hands and said goodbye. Jamie's dad put her on his back and carried her to the car, where she immediately fell asleep with a large grin on her face.

Reading Science

1. An author usually does some research before writing a text. What evidence of research can the reader find in this text?

   A. Jamie was beside herself that her dad finally agreed to take her to the zoo.

   B. Ben was a zoologist, who is a person who studies nocturnal animals.

   C. Jamie was also informed about how the porcupine sticks up its quills when it smells danger or a new smell.

   D. Upon arriving, Jamie was bug-eyed as she quietly gazed at the spotted owl.

2. What does the sentence, *She was beside herself that her dad had finally agreed*, imply to the reader?

   A. Jamie was standing beside herself.

   B. Jamie was elated about going to the zoo.

   C. Jamie was curious about what she would learn at the zoo.

   D. Jamie was standing beside her dad because he agreed to take her to the zoo.

Reading Science

3. What would be another appropriate title for this selection?

A. "Nocturnal Animals"

B. "Jamie's Nocturnal Night"

C. "Amazing Creatures"

D. "The Spotted Owl"

4. What evidence best supports the statement that animals have sense receptors that are specialized for particular types of information and processed by the animal's brain?

A. *"Unlike the owl, the red panda does not have the greatest hearing or eyesight."*

B. *Ben informed her by the tiger exhibit that cats grow whiskers as wide as their bodies. The whiskers help them know whether they will fit through spaces.*

C. *"Owls can't roll their eyes like humans."*

D. *"Owls can't roll their eyes like humans, which is why their heads are able to turn almost all the way around."*

5. What is the best summary of this selection?

A. Jamie and her dad went to the zoo at night. Ben, the tour guide, showed them the nocturnal animals. Jamie learned a large amount about how different animals use their sense receptors to be awake and hunt at night. Jamie loved her experience at the zoo.

B. Jamie learned about nocturnal animals by visiting the owls at the zoo. She learned that owls have elongated eye tubes and that red pandas are nocturnal. Jamie was so tired at the end that she fell asleep.

C. Ben, the tour guide, showed Jamie the owls. He explained to her that the owls have a keen sense of sight and hearing to help them hunt at night. Jamie asked many questions and learned about tigers, porcupines, and red pandas.

D. Jamie begged her dad to take her to the Nocturnal Nights experience at the zoo. Jamie's dad agreed. They went to the zoo, and Jamie was excited to learn about the animals. She learned that tigers have whiskers to help them gauge whether they will fit through a space. Jamie fell asleep from being up so late.

6. What identifies this story as realistic fiction?

A. The events that take place could really happen.

B. The author includes character dialogue.

C. The characters are people who are well-known.

D. The author asks questions throughout the story.

7. The author used the word **bug-eyed** to let the reader know–

    A.   Jamie's eyes could not close.

    B.   Jamie was extremely interested in and excited about the owls.

    C.   Jamie looked like a bug.

    D.   Jamie's eyes were big, like a bug's.

8. A synonym for the word **strode** in paragraph 11 is–

    A.   ran.

    B.   progressed.

    C.   jumped.

    D.   watched.

∞ Open-Ended Response

1. You accidentally touch the hot stove and burn your hand. How does remembering this experience help you?

_____

_____

_____

2. You are hungry. You walk into the kitchen and find your favorite meal cooking on the stove. How does your body respond to the messages your brain is receiving?

_____

_____

_____

_____

3. Can certain types of animals have stronger senses than others? Explain and give examples.

_____

_____

_____

_____

Claim-Evidence-Reasoning

Scenario:

Liam opened his pet frog's cage to put some crickets inside for the frog to eat. The frog became very still once the crickets were inside his cage. As soon as one came close enough, the frog shot out his tongue and gulped it up!

Prompt:

Write a scientific explanation describing the mental process of the frog and what caused it to act.

Claim:

_____

_____

_____

_____

_____

_____

_____

_____

_____

_____

_____

_____

_____

_____

_____

_____

Claim-Evidence-Reasoning

Evidence:

_____

_____

_____

_____

_____

_____

_____

Reasoning:

_____

_____

_____

_____

_____

_____

_____

_____

_____

_____

Plant and Animal Parts

Name: _____ Date: _____

Graphic Organizer

Plants and Animals

Directions

Both plants and animals have internal and external adaptations that help them survive, grow, behave, and reproduce. List these internal and external structures that plants and animals have.

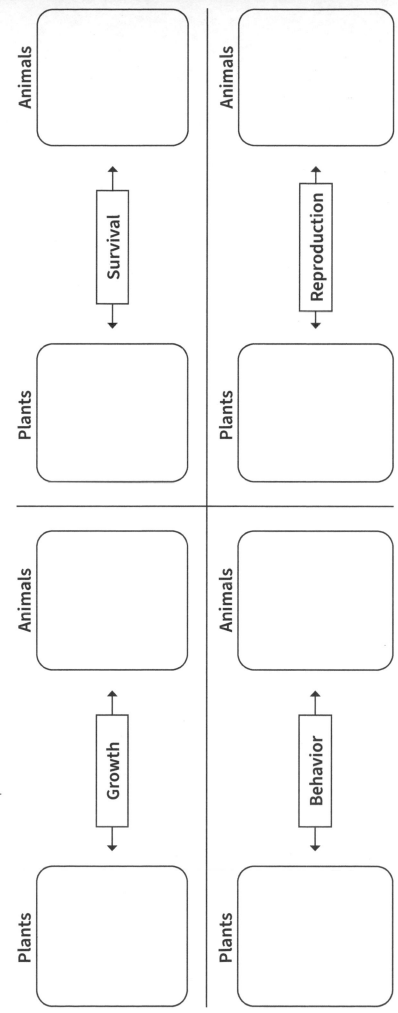

Plants → Growth → **Animals**

Animals ← Survival → **Plants**

Plants → Behavior → **Animals**

Animals ← Reproduction → **Plants**

Explore 1

Plant Guts

Draw the inside of two different fruits.

Fruit 1: _____	Fruit 2: _____

How are these fruits similar? _____

How are these fruits different? _____

Why are seeds important? _____

Part I: Investigating Stems

Draw the internal structure seen that allows water to travel through the plant. Show the path the water takes to get through the plant.

Explore 1

Create a bar graph to record your daily measurements of how far the color has traveled up the celery stalk.

Height of Color

Height (cm)

Day 1   Day 2   Day 3   Day 4

Reflection and Conclusion

1. As you observe the celery, what do you notice is happening?

_____

_____

2. What structures allowed the change in the celery to take place?

_____

_____

3. How do these structures support the plant's survival and growth?

_____

_____

Explore 1

Part II: Investigating Leaves

In the table below, record your observations of each flower for 3 days.

	Flower with NO Leaves (Draw a picture of the flower and write any observations you notice.)	Flower with Leaves (Draw a picture of the flower and write any observations you notice.)
Day 1		
Day 2		
Day 3		

Reflection and Conclusion

1. Which flower looks the healthiest at the end of Day 3?

_____

2. Why do you think leaves are important?

_____

_____

Explore 1

Plant Guts

Claim-Evidence-Reasoning

What is the function of the stem in a plant? Use scientific explanations in your reasoning.

Claim:

_____

_____

_____

Evidence:

_____

_____

_____

_____

Reasoning:

_____

_____

_____

_____

_____

_____

_____

_____

Explore 2

Interactive Model of Body Systems

Part I

Use the space below to illustrate the model your class created. Label each part and describe each process. Label the body structures that allow each system to function properly.

1. Which internal structure and body system played the biggest roles in the model? Explain.

_____

_____

_____

 **Explore 2**

2. What materials were taken to the muscular system, and which internal structure did they come from?

_____

_____

_____

3. What exchange was made at the muscular system?

_____

_____

_____

4. What allowed you to move through the model?

_____

_____

_____

5. Describe two moments when your body is getting rid of something it does not need.

_____

_____

_____

6. Summarize how the internal structures work together to form the systems of your body, enabling them to work together.

_____

_____

_____

_____

_____

Explore 2

Part II

1. What did you see when the black light was turned on? How did this happen?

_____

_____

_____

_____

_____

2. Which external structure helped prevent this substance from getting inside your body?

_____

_____

_____

_____

_____

3. What could you do to reduce the spread of germs?

_____

_____

_____

_____

_____

Explore 3

Adaptation Matchup

Explore 3

1. Why do adaptations occur? Why are they important?

_____

_____

_____

_____

_____

_____

2. What are some examples of plant and animal adaptations? How are they beneficial to the organism?

_____

_____

_____

_____

_____

_____

_____

3. What is likely to happen to an organism if it does not have the right adaptation for its environment?

_____

_____

_____

_____

_____

Linking Literacy
Pre-Reading

Ducks vs. Hummingbirds

Before you read: Look at the two birds below. Think about how they are similar and how they are different. Use the Venn diagram below to compare and contrast the two birds.

Linking Literacy
During-Reading

Internal and External Structures

While you read: Use the information in the text to help you identify the structure in each picture. Identify whether it is an internal or external structure and describe its function.

_____

_____

_____

_____

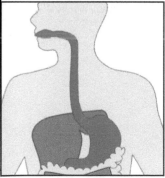

_____

_____

_____

_____

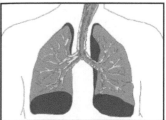

_____

_____

_____

_____

_____

_____

_____

Linking Literacy
Post-Reading

Plant and
Animal Parts

Describe the Adaptation

After you read: Look at the pictures of the two animals below. Describe the adaptations you
see and how you think they help the animal survive. Share your answers with your neighbor and
discuss what you think.

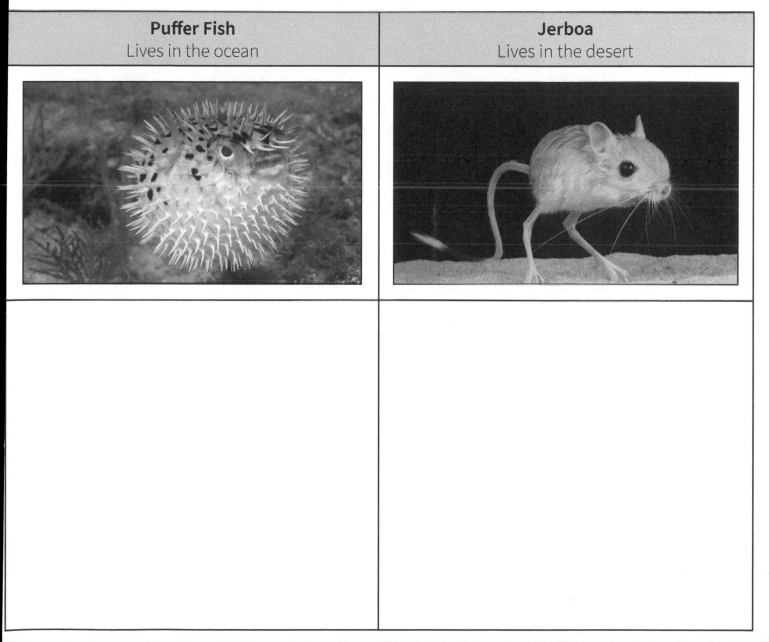

Puffer Fish Lives in the ocean	**Jerboa** Lives in the desert

Reading Science

Putting the Pieces Together: Plants

1. Living organisms, such as plants, animals, and humans, need energy to survive and grow. Every living organism has structures that help it survive in its environment. All the pieces have to be put together so the organism can grow, function, and survive.

Strong and Healthy

2. Some plants are known as *vascular plants*. Vascular plants have tubes that carry nutrients and water from the plant's roots. Roots are designed to pull water and minerals from whatever material in which they sit. Roots also hold the plant in place when wind occurs. Roots have root hairs. The hairs make the roots look fuzzy. They also absorb water and minerals.

3. Water and minerals are absorbed by the roots before they are carried up the stem and leaves. The stem's job is to carry food to the leaves. It also provides support for the plant. In some cases, it stores water.

4. The plant's leaves are filled with chloroplasts. Chloroplasts help the plant make energy and food through a process called *photosynthesis*. The plant must first take in sunlight to start photosynthesis. Once light has been absorbed, the plant takes in carbon dioxide and water. The plant changes the carbon dioxide and water into sugar. The vascular tubes carry the sugar to other parts of the plant. This sugar helps the plant grow from a seedling to an adult. As the plant produces food, it also releases oxygen. Oxygen is a gas needed by humans and animals.

Survival of the Fittest

5. Do all plants look the same? No, some plants have thick, waxy leaves to help them store water. You will find these plants in very warm climates, such as the desert. Other plants have long and twisty, vine-like leaf structures. Vine plants crawl to reach sunlight. You may find these kinds of plants in forests. Some plants have thorns. Nothing says "Don't eat me!" like a bunch of sharp thorns on your branches!

6. Some plants have no leaves. A cactus is an example of a plant with no leaves. A cactus is all stem and trunk, with no leaves. The cactus's trunk and stem allow it to **retain** water. Having no leaves means less water evaporation on hot days.

7. Some trees have bark to help them survive. Some bark is thick. It protects the tree from plants and insects. Other bark is meant to be peeled away as the tree grows.

8. Some plants grow on the side of trees. They have specialized root systems that help them **latch** on to larger objects. This way, they are able to collect water and nutrients from the tree. These plants are usually small. Some can be very large and weaken a tree. They can even make the tree die.

9. Finally, a plant's flowers help it survive. Some insects are attracted to certain colors of flowers. The scent that a flower gives off may not be attractive to some insects. The color and scent of flowers help the plant survive by attracting the right insects to the plant.

Making More Plants

10. Plants that rely on flowers for reproduction or more production of something need the help of insects to pollinate. Flowers make pollen. They use the pollen to make seeds that will eventually form another plant. A bee may land on a flower and get pollen on its back. It then goes to another flower, and the pollen may fall off the bee and land on the flower's stigma. Once pollinated, that flower will produce a fruit or seed.

11. Not all plants reproduce like flowers do. Some conifer plants use wind to reproduce by transferring pollen from one cone to another. Once the wind carries the pollen to the second cone, cells begin to make a baby conifer that lives in a seed.

12. Plants are very interesting. Every plant has important structures to help it grow, survive, and reproduce in its environment. Plants are important to our environment. Animals need plants to live! We need plants in more ways than one!

Reading Science

1. Which of the following would be an example of a conifer tree?

    A. Apple tree

    B. Pine tree

    C. Maple tree

    D. Flowering crab tree

2. Which of the following pieces of evidence helps the reader understand what the word **retain** means?

    A. *All stem and trunk*

    B. *On hot days*

    C. *Less water evaporation*

    D. *No leaves*

Reading Science

3. Which of the following is the best summary for this selection?

A. Plants have many means for survival. They can retain water or grow thorns to ward off predators. Plants can even reproduce with the help of bees.

B. Plants are capable of making their own food through photosynthesis. They are able to grow with the help of water and nutrients. Some plants, such as cacti, can retain water to help them survive. Flowering plants produce pollen to help them reproduce.

C. Plants have structures that help them grow. Plants are capable of making their own food, and this helps them grow. They also have special features that help them survive in their environments. Some plants reproduce with the help of bees to produce a seed and, eventually, a new plant.

D. Plants have structures that help them grow. Some plants are vascular and carry water and nutrients from their roots to their stems and, finally, to their leaves. The flower of the plant makes pollen, which is used in reproduction.

4. Which sentence(s) from the passage suggests that all living things need energy to live and grow?

A. *Once light has been absorbed, the plant takes in carbon dioxide and water. The plant changes the carbon dioxide and water into sugar.*

B. *They have specialized root systems that help them latch on to larger objects. This way, they are able to collect water and nutrients from the tree.*

C. *The vascular tubes carry the sugar to other parts of the plant. This sugar helps the plant grow from a seedling to an adult.*

D. *Chloroplasts help the plant make energy and food through a process called* photosynthesis.

Reading Science

5. How does the author use headings to help the reader gain information?

    A.   The headings give the reader facts about what they are about to read.

    B.   The headings help organize the author's information into different parts.

    C.   The headings help the reader know what the author was thinking.

    D.   The headings help the reader understand the title of the passage.

6. The author most likely wrote this passage to–

    A.   explain how plants produce energy to grow.

    B.   tell a story about a plant's life.

    C.   encourage readers to look more closely at plants.

    D.   describe the different structures of plants that help it grow, live, and survive.

Reading Science

7. Read the definitions for the word **latch** below.

latch\lach\noun

1. A device for holding a door or gate closed
2. To close or fasten with a latch
3. To take possession of
4. To grab or hold on

Which definition of **latch** is used in paragraph 8?

A.   Definition 1

B.   Definition 2

C.   Definition 3

D.   Definition 4

∞ Open-Ended Response

1. Frogs have internal and external structures to help them survive, grow, and reproduce. Name an internal and an external structure, and tell how these structures help the frog survive.

_____

_____

_____

_____

2. Bears are mammals with fur and lungs. How do these structures help a bear survive?

_____

_____

_____

_____

3. Explain how internal and external structures help a cactus plant survive in a desert environment.

_____

_____

_____

_____

Claim-Evidence-Reasoning

Scenario:

The lion was breathing fast and her heart was racing as she chased after the wildebeest. She caught up to it, took one giant leap, grabbed the back of the wildebeest with her sharp claws, and pulled it down to the ground. The wildebeest fought back. It swung its horns at the lion and tried to stomp on her with its hooves. The lion eventually won the battle and ate her prey.

Prompt:

Write a scientific explanation describing how the lion's internal and external structures were useful.

Claim:

_____

_____

_____

_____

_____

Claim-Evidence-Reasoning

Evidence:

_____

_____

_____

_____

_____

_____

_____

Reasoning:

_____

_____

_____

_____

_____

_____

_____

_____

_____

Light Reflection

Graphic Organizer

How Do I See?

Directions

In each arrow, write the process that describes how we are able to see each of the objects.

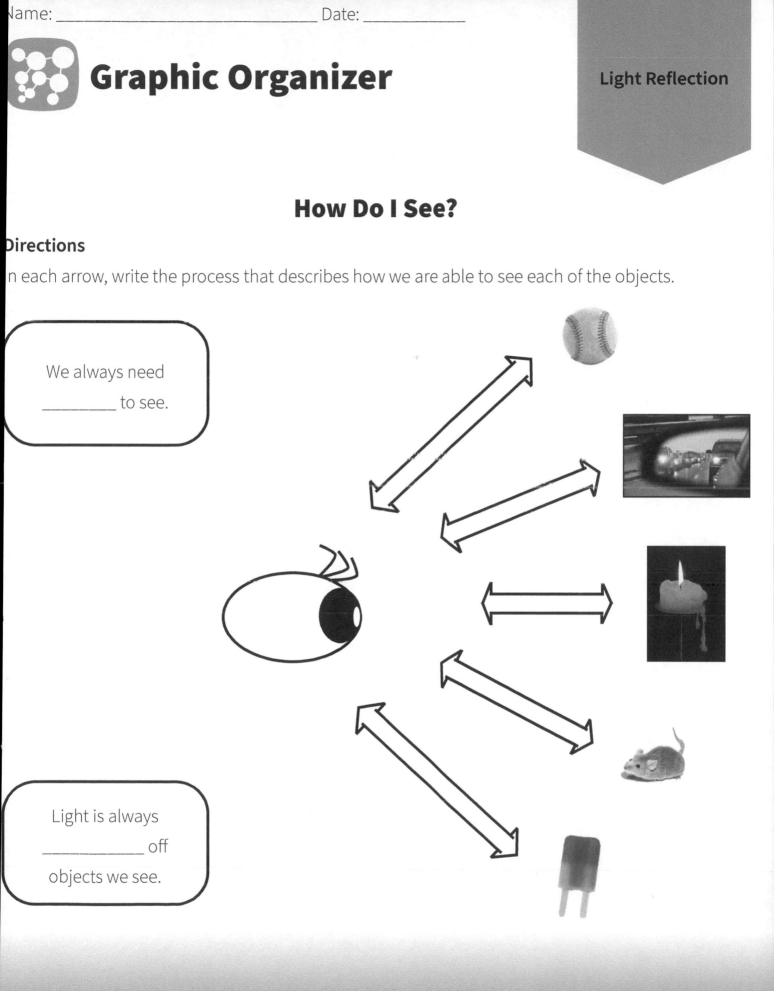

We always need
_____ to see.

Light is always
_____ off
objects we see.

Explore 1

Bull's-Eye!

Directions

Draw and label how your team got the penlight to hit the bull's-eye. Be sure to include where the mirrors were and draw the path of light.

One Mirror	Two Mirrors	Three Mirrors

1. How does light travel?

_____

_____

2. What happened to the path of light when you used the mirrors?

_____

_____

3. What allowed you to see your light on the bull's-eye?

_____

_____

_____

Explore 1

Bulls-Eye!

Claim-Evidence-Reasoning

Using scientific reasoning, explain how light travels.

Claim:

_____
_____
_____

Evidence:

_____
_____
_____

Reasoning:

_____
_____
_____
_____
_____
_____

Explore 2

Let There Be Light!

1. What is light, and how does it help us see?

_____

_____

2. Look through the hole in your box. Do not remove the lid. Draw exactly what you see in the space below.

Closed Shoe box

3. What do you think is inside the box?

_____

_____

Explore 2

4. Lift the lid on your shoe box and look inside. Draw exactly what you see in the space below.

Open Shoe box

5. What is inside the box?

_____

_____

6. What caused you to be able to see the object better?

_____

_____

7. What path is the light taking?

_____

_____

Explore 2

Let There Be Light!

Claim-Evidence-Reasoning

Using scientific reasoning, explain why it was easier to see the object in an open shoe box.

Claim:

_____

_____

_____

Evidence:

_____

_____

_____

_____

Reasoning:

_____

_____

_____

_____

_____

_____

Explore 3

Periscope

The Problem

Your teacher has hidden an object behind a "wall" on your desk.

The Challenge

Use the mirrors and cardboard rolls to create a model that allows you to see what object is behind your wall.

Criteria and Constraints

- You may only use the materials provided by the teacher.
- Your device should allow you to see around the wall while you are standing on the other side of it.
- You may not look on the other side of the wall.
- You must design your device by creating a labeled blueprint before building it.

Brainstorm and Research

Write down any ideas you have about how you could master the challenge. If you need more information, write down what you need to know and gain permission from your teacher to research the answer.

Explore 3

Design Plan

Use the ideas you wrote down while brainstorming to develop a final design plan. Draw your plan and label the parts. Be sure to list what each part is made of.

Build and Test

Build your design and test it. Does it meet all the criteria and constraints? Use the space below to list what problems you need to fix in your design.

Refine and Redesign

How could you solve the problems you found during testing? Use the space below to draw your new design that should solve the problems.

Explore 3

Retest and Finalize

Build and test your new design. Does it meet all the criteria and constraints? If not, repeat the refine and redesign process. If so, move on to planning your presentation.

Presentation Plan

Use the space below to plan how you will present your final product. Be sure to include who will speak and what you want to say. Your presentation should include the scientific ideas used to solve this design challenge.

Linking Literacy
Pre-Reading

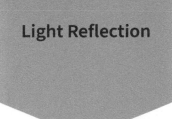

Sources of Light

Directions: Use the table below to record observations about each source of light you observe. Then draw a picture of the objects.

Source of Light	Illustration

Linking Literacy
During-Reading

Note-Taking Guide

Directions: Use this page to take notes below while you read.

1. How We See Light

   a. An object can be seen when _____
   _____.

   b. The light that an object does not absorb is reflected back as visible light and received by the _____.

   c. Our eyes absorb light waves and transmit the _____
   to the _____ to be _____.

   d. The brain processes the waves as _____.

2. How Do Mirrors Work?

   a. We see light bounce off the mirror's _____ and reflect what is in front of it.

   b. The first mirrors were made of a stone called _____.

   c. The Greeks and Romans used highly polished _____
   and _____ for mirrors.

   d. Mirrors are now made with very _____ sheets of _____.

3. The Angles of Mirrors

    a.   When light strikes a mirror at an angle, it reflects the _____ angle.

In the space below, write two facts you found interesting in the reading. If you still have any questions about mirrors, write them in the space below.

1.

2.

_____

_____

_____

_____

Linking Literacy
Post-Reading

Four-Corner Summary

Copy the following onto a note card. Using the text or notes from the text, write four facts about the center topic. Then turn each fact into a sentence, forming a paragraph on the back of the note card.

FACT

FACT

Light Reflection

FACT

FACT

📖 Reading Science

Rainbows

1. A rainbow can be a beautiful sight after a storm. Kids may run outside and point to it. Adults may stop their work to gaze at it. Poets may feel inspired to write about it. In short, many people feel hope when they see a rainbow.

2. To scientists, however, rainbows are events that demonstrate the characteristics of light—refraction and reflection.

3. The ingredients for a rainbow are simple and common. It only takes sunlight and water droplets to make a rainbow. These ingredients need to be arranged just right, meaning the sunlight must hit the water at the proper angle. Water droplets in the air are almost perfect spheres. As light passes through a drop of water, the light changes its speed and refracts, or bends. This refraction causes the light to separate into colors. You see, light appears to be white to our eyes, but it is actually composed of all the colors of the rainbow. Refraction allows us to see those colors.

4. When the colors of light separate, they always separate the same way. The colors are always arranged in the same order: red, orange, yellow, green, blue, indigo, and violet. Violet, or purple, is always on the inside curve of the primary rainbow.

5. The sunlight that is refracted inside the water droplet is reflected off the back of the droplet. The back of the droplet acts like a mirror. It reflects the rainbow colors back, so we can see them.

6. Sometimes, we see two rainbows. The primary rainbow is the inner arch and is the brightest. The secondary rainbow is a mirror image (the colors are reversed) and dimmer than the primary. A double rainbow is a very special display.

7. A rare variation of the rainbow is the moonbow, or lunar rainbow. Moonbows take place at night. They are composed of the same colors as ordinary rainbows, but it is hard for human eyes to **perceive**, or see, the colors in the dim light. For this reason, moonbows appear white to the naked eye. When a special camera is used, however, the colors can be visible in a photograph.

8. To see these properties for yourself, you can create a rainbow in your own yard. Using a hose, make a fine spray of water. Your back should be to the Sun, so the light will reflect off the back of the droplets toward you. This smaller rainbow will appear to be just like the larger version found in the sky.

9. We can learn a great deal about light from rainbows, but we can also enjoy them. Refraction and reflection paint the sky more splendidly than an artist paints a masterpiece.

Reading Science

1. How do scientists think differently about rainbows than most people?

   A. Scientists are not excited when they see rainbows.

   B. Scientists think it is silly to try to learn anything from rainbows.

   C. Scientists can learn a large amount of information about light from rainbows.

   D. Scientists wish they could write poems about rainbows.

2. The back of a water droplet acts as a mirror. When light hits the water droplet, it bounces back to our eyes. This is called–

   A. refraction.

   B. evaporation.

   C. conduction.

   D. reflection.

3. The word **perceive** in this passage (paragraph 7) means–

   A. think about.

   B. read.

   C. see.

   D. understand.

4. Complete the following analogy:

   Moon is to moonbow as _____ is to rainbow.

   A. water

   B. the Sun

   C. sky

   D. Earth

Reading Science

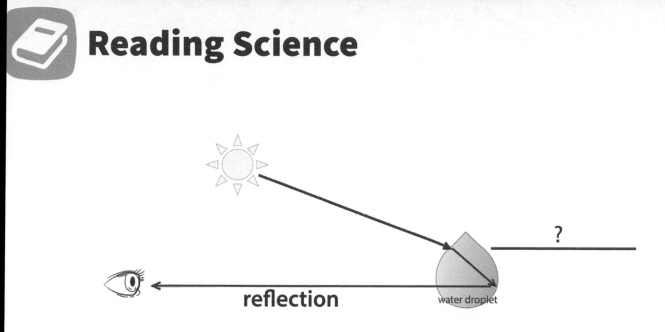

reflection

water droplet

5. Which of following words should replace the question mark in the diagram?

A. Refraction

B. Reflection

C. Light energy

D. Rainbow

∞ Open-Ended Response

1. How can you use a flashlight and mirror to demonstrate reflection?

_____

_____

_____

_____

2. A boy was riding in a car and noticed a small spot of light moving around on the ceiling of the car. He looked around and noticed the Sun was shining on his watch. Provide an explanation for why he saw the spot on the ceiling. Do you think he would see this spot every day? Why?

_____

_____

_____

_____

3. Thoroughly explain why you are able to see the objects around you.

_____

_____

_____

_____

Claim-Evidence-Reasoning

Scenario:

Jarrel and Tony were on a cave tour during their vacation. They used flashlights to look at a stream of water flowing down one of the cave walls. Jarrel moved a little closer to get a better look and tripped over a rock. He said, "Ouch! Where did that rock come from? I couldn't see it!"

Prompt:

Use scientific reasoning to explain why Jarrel did not see the rock.

Claim:

_____

_____

_____

_____

_____

_____

Claim-Evidence-Reasoning

Evidence:

_____

_____

_____

_____

_____

_____

_____

Reasoning:

_____

_____

_____

_____

_____

_____

_____

_____

_____

_____

_____

_____

Information Technologies

Graphic Organizer

Today's Technology

Directions

Pick four forms of technology used today. Explain how each transmits data or a voice. Explain what the end result is.

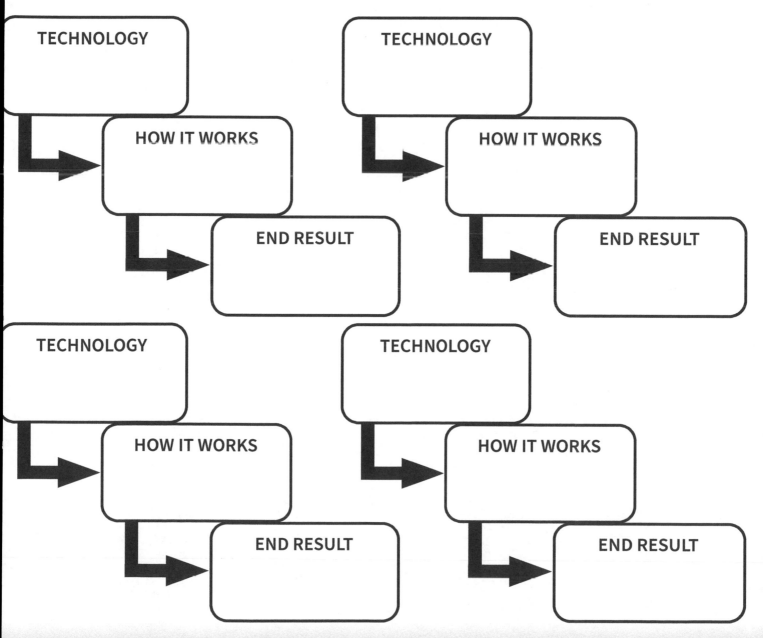

TECHNOLOGY

HOW IT WORKS

END RESULT

TECHNOLOGY

HOW IT WORKS

END RESULT

TECHNOLOGY

HOW IT WORKS

END RESULT

TECHNOLOGY

HOW IT WORKS

END RESULT

Explore 1

Hidden Messages

You will be given a Semaphore Flags Code sheet and a Braille Code sheet. You will be assigned a code before you begin. Use the space provided to make notes and record your code. Put away the code sheet you will not be using. Quickly and quietly decipher the code. Solve it quietly so other groups do not hear the answer.

Semaphore Code	Braille Code
What does the code say?	**What does the code say?**
_____ _____ _____ _____ _____	_____ _____ _____ _____ _____

Explore 1

1. What were the similarities in patterns used to transfer information using both these codes?

_____

_____

_____

_____

2. What are the differences in patterns used to transfer information using both these codes?

_____

_____

_____

_____

Explore 1

Hidden Messages

Claim-Evidence-Reasoning

Write a scientific explanation for the similarities and differences between semaphore and Braille codes.

Claim:

_____

_____

_____

Evidence:

_____

_____

_____

_____

Reasoning:

_____

_____

_____

_____

_____

Explore 2

How Does It Work?

Directions:

You and your group members will be rotating through various stations. When you get to a station, read the procedure steps and answer the questions.

Station I: Sending Text

1. Look at the page 3. This is the alphabet converted to binary code. Binary code is a series of numbers that are converted to letters to form messages. Let's explore binary code!

2. Go to your favorite search engine.

3. In the search bar, type "convert text to binary code."

4. Choose from one of the multiple sites.

5. Go to the site and type in a word of your choosing. What word did you choose?

_____

6. Record the binary code the computer converts it to.

_____

7. Describe the speed of how long it took to convert your text to binary code.

_____

8. Type a few sentences for the computer to convert to binary code. Write your sentences in the space below.

_____

9. Highlight and copy the binary code. Ask your teacher to show you how to do this step if you are having difficulty.

Explore 2

10. Open a new web browser. Go to your favorite search engine again, and in the search bar type, "convert binary code to text."

11. Choose from one of the multiple sites.

12. Go to the site and paste your binary code.

13. Click back and choose a different converter site. Again, paste your binary code.

14. What happened on both sites when you pasted your binary code?

Explore 2

Alphabet to Binary Code

Lowercase Letters		Uppercase Letters	
a	01100001	A	01000001
b	01100010	B	01000010
c	01100011	C	01000011
d	01100100	D	01000100
e	01100101	E	01000101
f	01100110	F	01000110
g	01100111	G	01000111
h	01101000	H	01001000
i	01101001	I	01001001
j	01101010	J	01001010
k	01101011	K	01001011
l	01101100	L	01001100
m	01101101	M	01001101
n	01101110	N	01001110
o	01101111	O	01001111
p	01110000	P	01010000
q	01110001	Q	01010001
r	01110010	R	01010010
s	01110011	S	01010011
t	01110100	T	01010100
u	01110101	U	01010101
v	01110110	V	01010110
w	01110111	W	01010111
x	01111000	X	01011000
y	01111001	Y	01011001
z	01111010	Z	01011010

Explore 2

Station 2: Radio Waves

1. Watch your teacher point the remote at you and press buttons. What do you see?

_____

_____

2. Draw or explain what you saw when your teacher pointed the remote at the digital camera.

3. What do you think the remote is doing when it flickers?

_____

_____

_____

Station 3: Sending Images

1. Take two sheets of grid paper. One should have larger squares and one should have small squares.

2. On the grid paper with large squares, choose one simple thing to draw by shading in the squares. You can only shade in a square completely or leave it completely blank. Make the shape the best you can by coloring in squares.

Explore 2

. Glue your grid paper in the space below.

. Repeat the same shape on the grid paper with smaller squares. Glue your grid paper in the space below.

. On which size of grid paper was your image clearer?

Explore 2

Explore 3

Secret Code

The Problem

You have an idea for a new high-tech device that will be able to digitize and transmit messages that are created by the movement of your eyes. You are afraid an employee might steal your idea during your discussion with the president of a company that will make the high-tech device prototype. You are afraid other people can decipher the codes that already exist, so you decide to create a new code that will allow you to send a message to the prototype company about how information technologies work.

The Challenge

Create a code and send a message about what your group learned about information technologies.

Criteria and Constraints

Your message must be approved by the teacher and be at least one complete sentence.

Your code can be numbers, symbols, pictures, or colors.

Your code should be shared with another group to see if they can crack it.

Your message must discuss something learned regarding the transfer of information.

Brainstorm and Research

Write down any ideas you have about how you could master the challenge. If you need more information, write down what you need to know and gain permission from your teacher to research the answer.

 **Explore 3**

Design Plan

Use the ideas you wrote down while brainstorming to develop a final design plan. Draw your plan and label the parts. Be sure to list what each part is made of.

Build and Test

Build your design and test it. Does it meet all the criteria and constraints? Use the space below to list what problems you need to fix in your design.

Refine and Redesign

How could you solve the problems you found during testing? Use the space below to draw your new design that should solve the problems.

Explore 3

Retest and Finalize

Build and test your new design. Does it meet all the criteria and constraints? If not, repeat the refine and redesign process. If so, move on to planning your presentation.

Presentation Plan

Use the space below to plan how you will present your final product. Be sure to include who will speak and what you want to say. Your presentation should include the scientific ideas used to solve this design challenge.

Name: _____ Date: _____

Linking Literacy
Pre-Reading

Technology Brainstorm

Use this page to brainstorm the different technologies you use in your daily life. You only have three minutes, so write quickly!

Linking Literacy
During-Reading

Concept Mapping

Directions: While reading, choose four types of information technology that have influenced our world. List details about each type of technology from the text.

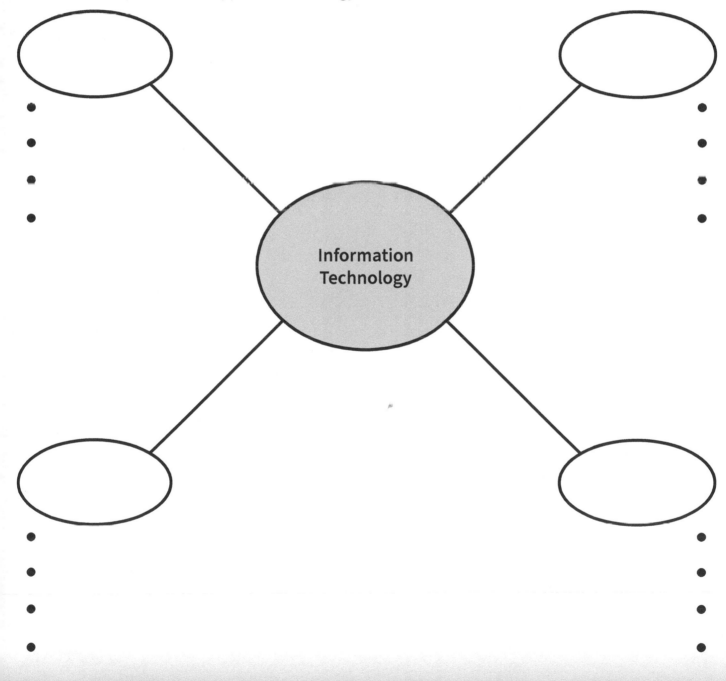

Linking Literacy
Post-Reading

Walk Around Paragraph

Write a sentence that answers the prompt. On your teacher's signal, move to another student's paper, read his or her sentence, and write a sentence elaborating on his or her thought. The process will continue until you have written an entire paragraph.

How have information technologies changed our lives?

Sentence one answers the prompt:

In addition . . .

Also . . .

Finally . . .

📖 Reading Science

Technology

Technology is all around you. People are on their cell phones everywhere. They use them for sending email and text messages. People make phone calls, surf the Internet, and play games on cell phones. Many people have cell phones. Some kids have cell phones, too!

Cell phones are not connected to your house. You can use them inside or outside. Using a cell phone, you can make a call at the park, the beach, or the grocery store. Cell phones are important. They let us keep in touch with our family. They also let us make emergency phone calls.

A cell phone is a kind of radio. Radio waves are in the air and around us all the time. We can't see radio waves. A cell phone uses battery power to send and receive signals on radio waves.

There is a tiny computer in a cell phone. It sends signals to the nearest base station. A base station has a tall, steel tower. There are antennas on the tower. These send and receive radio wave signals. The signals go from tower to tower. Then, they go from cell phone to cell phone.

Cell phones work well when they are near towers. Callers then have a better chance of having a clear-sounding conversation. If a cell phone is farther away from a tower, it is possible that the call may not sound as clear. The call may break up or be dropped.

Smartphones are another type of cellular device that people use today. They are just like cell phones but have a few differences. The main difference is that smartphones can process data. Data processing lets you send and receive email, text messages, pictures, and videos. Cell phone data networks process information for video chat, such as Skype and FaceTime.

7. When you send a text, it goes to a data tower. The data tower acts like an antenna. When the text reaches the data tower, it is moved to another data tower. It continues this pattern until it reaches a tower that is close to the person you are trying to contact. You want more towers between you and a friend for clearer data **transmission**. This will allow your friend to view a clear video.

8. Imagine you are at the mall and have a question; you can check the Internet. You pull out your smartphone. You check the Internet. When you use the Internet, your phone sends a signal to the data tower that you want to use the Internet. The data tower sends the signal to the Internet. Your phone pulls up the World Wide Web, and you can search to find your answer.

9. Smartphones and cell phones help us keep in touch with our family and friends near and far. Thanks to the smartphone and cell phone, we can connect in ways we could not many years ago.

Reading Science

. The author's way of organizing this passage helps the reader understand–

   A.   the steps of how a phone call is made.

   B.   how a cell phone works.

   C.   the differences between cell phones and smartphones.

   D.   how cell phones have changed our world.

. The main message of paragraph 8 describes–

   A.   how smartphones connect to the Internet.

   B.   the purposes of a smartphone.

   C.   how smartphones answer questions.

   D.   how smartphones can be used anywhere.

Reading Science

3. Which statement best supports the idea that cell phones have infinite possibilities?

    A. *Cell phones are different because they are not connected to your house.*

    B. *A cell phone is a kind of radio.*

    C. *People use cell phones for sending email and text messages, making phone calls, surfing the Internet, or even playing games.*

    D. *Smartphones are another type of cellular device that people use today.*

4. What does the word **transmission** mean in this passage?

    A. Moving from one location to another

    B. A connection

    C. A force

    D. A system of shafts and gears

Reading Science

. If the reader were to place a heading before paragraph 6, what would it be?

A. "The Internet"

B. "How Cell Phones Work"

C. "How Smartphones Work"

D. "Get a Smartphone"

. In order for a cell phone or smartphone to work, there must be–

A. a person on the other end to receive the call.

B. a series of cellular towers to intercept the signal.

C. a person at the cell phone company to connect your phone.

D. a working Internet connection.

7. How is a smartphone like a computer?

A. It can connect to the Internet.

B. It can be used to Skype or FaceTime your friends near and far.

C. It can send email to others.

D. All of the above

∞ Open-Ended Response

Why is it important to be able to transmit information over long distances?

_____

_____

_____

_____

Explain how you could share a message with a friend sitting across the room without talking.

_____

_____

_____

_____

Describe two real-world examples in which people use digitized information to communicate.

_____

_____

_____

_____

Claim-Evidence-Reasoning

Scenario:

Communications can be sent in many different ways. In Africa, New Guinea, and tropical America, people have used drum telegraphy to communicate with each other from far away for centuries. Native Americans used smoke signals from their fire. Others used a telegraph machine to produce short and long sounds, called Morse code. Morse code was used later by submarines with flashing lights. A cell phone turns your voice into a signal that is transmitted via radio waves to a nearby cell tower. The tower sends your voice to the person you are calling within milliseconds. Information, including pictures, graphs, and charts, can also be transmitted with cell phones.

Fire outposts are often used in the mountains of Colorado to watch for deadly forest fires. Fire outposts are equipped with emergency supplies, including a cell tower, flashlights, and a telegraph machine with a manual. Forest rangers working at an outpost notice flames about 100 miles east of the tower. When they try to call the ranger's station, their call won't go through. Further investigation shows that the cell tower has been damaged. If they don't get word to the ranger's station soon, the town on the other side of the mountains could be destroyed. It will take too long to drive the winding road down to the station. The smoke in the sky is starting to get thick, and they have to think fast.

Prompt:

Write a scientific explanation describing which type of communication device at the fire outpost is best for the scenario above.

Claim-Evidence-Reasoning

Claim:

_____

_____

_____

_____

Evidence:

_____

_____

_____

_____

Reasoning:

_____

_____

_____

_____

_____

_____

_____

_____